FIERY (BUT MOSTLY PEACEFUL)

FIERY (BUT MOSTLY PEACEFUL)

THE 2020 RIOTS AND THE GASLIGHTING OF AMERICA

JULIO ROSAS

ISBN: 978-1-956007-02-2

Cover design by David Fassett
First Edition

Published by DW Books
DW Books is a division of Daily Wire

Daily Wire
1831 12th Avenue South
Suite 460
Nashville, TN 37203

www.dailywire.com

PRINTED IN THE USA

CONTENTS

1

"It's Not, Generally Speaking, Unruly"

WAKING on the morning of Tuesday, May 26, 2020, in Los Angeles, where I was sheltering from COVID-19 with family, I performed the a.m. ritual of the 21st-century journalist: I immediately reached for my phone to check Twitter.

The social-media platform was blowing up, consumed with outrage over an incident in Minnesota the evening before.

Furiously making the rounds were videos of a white Minneapolis police officer, Derek Chauvin, kneeling on the neck of a black man named George Floyd for nearly ten minutes.

The videos showed onlookers begging Chauvin to stop; Floyd, under arrest for allegedly passing a counterfeit $20 bill, was already in handcuffs and said he was having trouble breathing. Making matters worse, the videos showed three other Minneapolis police officers standing by watching, doing nothing to intervene.

Floyd was pronounced dead at the Hennepin County Medical Center an hour later.

Right away I knew there were going to be protests—and possibly riots—over the incident. Still, I thought these would take time to develop because, I believed, people would be reluctant to gather in large groups over COVID-19 fears.

I was wrong. That very night in Minneapolis, as news about Floyd's death spread, protests broke out with angry mobs flooding the streets. These soon turned violent.

Protesters initially gathered at the 3rd Police Precinct, where Chauvin and the other officers involved in the Floyd incident had been assigned. (All four were fired the day after Floyd's death.)

The situation quickly spiraled out of control, with some protesters sparking fights with officers. Police used tear gas, rubber bullets, and flashbangs in futile attempts to control order. Rioters, meanwhile, broke into the precinct motor pool and began destroying police vehicles.

By Wednesday night, crowds again gathered at the 3rd Precinct. Tensions, already high, soared further. Looting and rioting spread to nearby businesses: An AutoZone, a Wendy's, and an apartment complex serving low-income families were all set on fire.

Local news showed looters ransacking the Target across the street from the 3rd Precinct—a particular irony since Target's corporate headquarters are based in Minneapolis, and the corporation is heavily identified with the Twin Cities.

Watching the videos of buildings being set ablaze made me realize this was not going to be like anything I had covered before.

I needed to get on the ground in the Twin Cities as quickly as possible.

I hardly slept the night before my flight, my mind racing with worry thinking about the maelstrom into which I was about to be dropped.

MAY 28TH

Getting to the Minneapolis-St. Paul airport was the easy part, of course. Getting from the airport to the epicenter of the unfolding chaos was going to be a lot harder.

Luckily, a friend of a friend, a Twin Cities native named Jon, agreed to act as my guide. Picking me up from the airport, Jon gave me the lay of the land and tips of potential places rioters could hit next. We decided to head to the area of the 3rd Precinct.

My first stop after getting dropped off was the heavily looted and damaged Target. Graffiti covered the outside of the building, with messages ranging from "Fuck 12" (slang for "Fuck the police") and "Cops did this" to "RIP George" and "Fire to the pigs."

The store's sprinklers, activated by the smoke from the nearby fires, had left several inches of water on the floor before shutting off, though a busted sprinkler in the clothing section continued showering water down from the ceiling. Thankfully my Gortex boots kept my feet dry.

The fire alarm blared loudly and would continue to blare until at least that Saturday. Only the emergency lights on the ceiling were on, giving the store a dark, creepy post-apocalyptic vibe.

The floor was littered with items that had been thrown from the shelves. Snacks, books, binders, holiday cards, small handheld American flags, and anything the first wave of looters had deemed not worth stealing covered the floor, creating large, soggy piles of trash. The store smelled of what I could only describe as wet, burnt cigarettes.

People were still going in and out of Target and picking over what had initially been left behind, but little of value remained.

I walked by the grocery section of the store. Refrigerator and freezer doors were left open, though I think it would not have mattered since it looked as though some were no longer working, and many items were still inside. I saw pints of Ben & Jerry's ice cream and, for a brief moment, thought of taking one since it would be a waste of ice cream to let it melt. (What can I say? I have a sweet tooth.) I quickly decided against taking a pint since the freezer door had been left open for who knows how long.

At the store's checkout area, looters had torn open the bottom sections of the self-checkout lanes to get to the cash and change underneath. Registers had been thrown to the ground. Target's Starbucks location was also heavily damaged, its windows smashed. Curious onlookers peeked in from the sidewalk to take their own photos and videos.

Throughout the area, wearing a mask was prudent, but not necessarily for COVID-19. There was still so much smoke in the air from the smoldering ash piles where buildings had once stood that not wearing a mask would quickly result in a fit of sneezes and coughs.

In stark contrast to the looting, there were locals trying to clean up the mess from the night before in the parking lot of the strip mall. As I was posting videos of the scene on Twitter, people mainly had one question: Where were the police?

It was a good question.

The Minneapolis Police largely remained holed up in the 3rd Precinct's main building as crowds gathered. While the crowd's anger was palpable—calls of "Fuck the police! Fuck 'em!" were heard frequently—the protests *were* mostly peaceful, at least during the day. Not to say there weren't fights, but they were largely confined to infighting among the protesters. Protesters took it upon themselves to direct traffic to ensure cars did not drive through the crowds gathered outside the 3rd Precinct. One driver rolled down his window after being turned around to talk to one of the ad hoc traffic cops. Before the driver could say a word, the protester began shouting: "Do you feel inconvenienced? You're part of the problem! You're pissed off that I gotta turn you around!"

"No, I'm trying to support you guys," the driver tried to explain.

"Then get out of your car!" the protester screamed. "Park your car right here! Get out!"

When the driver said he was not going to leave his car in the middle of the street, the protester got angrier. "Why? Because your possessions are worth more than people's lives? Get the fuck out of here! Get the fuck out of here!"

At the perimeter of the precinct itself, which had a fence around it, one black man told the crowd that while he appreciated white people showing up to give their support, "this is not your space." The reason they were wary of white people showing up, particularly those affiliated with Antifa/black bloc groups, he explained, is because they did not want them to start fights with the police since it would give the officers an excuse to respond with force.

The only time I saw Minneapolis police outside the precinct's perimeter on Thursday was when a convoy of SUVs and vans rolled down the street parallel to the Target and the Cub Foods grocery store. The crowd was unhappy at the police presence. Some started throwing all sorts of projectiles at the officers, from rocks to empty Hennessy bottles. Police responded with tear gas, rubber bullets, pepper balls, and flashbangs.

Things became more heated after someone from the crowd was arrested for stabbing a protester, according to an Australian news crew that was nearby. Officers dismounted to give first aid to a person who appeared to have been hit with a crowd control munition and to transport him from the area.

Even with the officers trying to help, they still encountered resistance from the crowd, who wanted an ambulance, and not police, to take the person away.

"The ambulance is not coming here!" an officer told screaming protesters.

The cops had to use pepper spray after one young man got into a shoving match with an officer, and I was caught in the cloud. Once the injured individual was loaded into one of the vans, the convoy began to pull away. Even though one of their own was in a police vehicle, rioters in the crowd continued to throw objects at the vehicles, which made recording what was happening a challenge.

Obviously, getting close to the police convoy was not an option, but since not all the rioters had pitching arms that could have gotten them into the Major Baseball League, I had to constantly move alongside the convoy to avoid getting hit from behind by objects that fell short of their intended target. Minneapolis Police deployed tear gas to cover their exit, which was promptly thrown back at them by the rioters.

Still recording the confrontations, I slid down a small berm that was near the sidewalk and sat down, trying to lay low. After I finished recording a video, I could see an officer in an SUV with the window rolled down, looking in my direction. Through my phone screen, I saw him point a pepper ball gun right at me. I shook my head no, but he shot a pepper ball at my upper left thigh. Coughing and slightly disoriented, I got up and began to walk away. At that point the police convoy was able to leave quickly, with the crowd following them as they viewed themselves the victors in the skirmish.

After following the crowd for some time, I went back to the strip mall in search of a signal to upload videos. Coming from the north end, I saw some Somali men standing outside a cafe that belonged to one of them. "People were trying to break in," they told me, adding that other minority-owned businesses that belonged to Asians and Hispanics had also been targeted by rioters the night before.

It wasn't just big-name stores that were being damaged or destroyed. One restaurant right across the street from the 3rd Precinct had "Minority owned business" graffitied on its windows. It was largely untouched throughout Thursday, but the liquor and tobacco stores next door were ransacked.

The area became somewhat peaceful again once the police convoy left. The Target's parking lot had been turned into a supply stash point for protesters. Food, water, and medical supplies taken from the Target and Cub Foods grocery store were put into one area for people to grab as much as they wanted. For miles, there were almost no businesses that were open. I had barely eaten all day, and I was already running out of water; I had no choice but to take supplies from the stash. I had been so used to protests and violent confrontations not affecting the miles around the scene that

I realized just how underprepared I was for this moment. I then began to see why people felt the need to loot the grocery store in this extreme circumstance.

Going into St. Paul was out of the question. Looting was beginning to occur there as well, coincidentally starting at another Target. Public transportation and ride sharing apps had all but evaporated, making travel throughout the Twin Cities difficult or downright impossible for anyone without access to a car.

I could see why someone, seeing the closed businesses and rampant destruction, would feel the need to secure as much food as possible since they wouldn't know when stores would reopen and be restocked. I understood taking food and other staples from the shelves. And I have a real sympathy for those who were concerned about taking care of their families in such uncertain circumstances.

Of course, this understanding stops at those who loot materialistic items, especially at the expense of small business owners, since those are not needed for the immediate survival of oneself or one's family. Regular people were put into that position because others wanted to take advantage of the anger and lawlessness.

Inside the Cub Foods was eerily similar to the nearby Target. People flowed in and out, often taking the carts to help carry away large numbers of items. Piles of discarded products littered the floor. Towards the front of the store, a group of people was trying to smash open the ATM. I don't know if they ever did get it open; I left after watching them struggle unsuccessfully for some time.

To be clear, this is not a defense of looting. It's to highlight how the basic tenets of a civilized society in Minneapolis had broken down so much and so quickly that it made some people desperate to do things they normally would not have done.

Most of the protesters had proclaimed the area to be a waypoint for tolerance and justice. But not all were welcomed. A church group had arrived at the Target's parking lot and began singing worship songs. Since the leader was a white woman and they appeared to be of a Christian denomination, some in the crowd began to heckle the group.

"Get the fuck outta here!" one man shouted. "Go the fuck home! Go home! Get your white savior complex outta here! No one asked for your help!"

"Give the mic to a fucking black person!" another shouted.

One person walked up and pulled the cords from the group's guitars' amplifiers. Another person came up behind the church group's guitar player and started to mess with his tuning keys.

The church leader tried to ease tensions by taking a knee to show solidarity. This only made some protesters angrier, believing she was trying to take the focus off Floyd's death. While all of this was going on, a car was burning behind them in the Target's parking lot.

It was starting to get dark at this point. The type of people in the crowd was noticeably changing. Gone were the older members of the community who wore medical face masks to protect against COVID-19 and the burning embers from the nearby buildings. In their place were younger people, dressed in almost all black or dark clothing, and wearing black or red bandanas on their faces. It was a more menacing crowd. One white man, who wore dark clothing Antifa agitators typically wear, had used bolt cutters to cut holes in the 3rd Precinct fence so people could infiltrate the perimeter.

I had been in contact with FOX News host Laura Ingraham's production crew to report live from the scene. I had never done an on-scene segment before, and I was hoping to give a smooth report.

"At least things are still calm," I had said to the producer in advance.

About twenty minutes before I was supposed to appear on her show, the night's violence erupted. The crowd, larger in number, started to shake and pull down the fencing around the 3rd Precinct.

At this point, the officers who had been on the roof all day observing the crowd were nowhere to be seen. Once the fence at the front entrance was torn down and objects were being thrown at the building, the officers on the roof reappeared and began to fire less-than-lethal ordnance at the rioters.

"I ain't running from nothing!" one rioter shouted. Seconds later a flashbang went off, and he quickly changed his tune. He and others, myself included, ran away from the fence.

I bolted across the street towards the burned-down AutoZone, where I was supposed to meet with the FOX News crew. They weren't there. Rioters then began building makeshift barricades in the street for cover so they could throw projectiles at the officers on the roof from close proximity. The acrid smell of tear gas and the sounds of flashbangs and fireworks filled the air.

I called the cameraman to find where they were. "Are we still on for the hit?" I asked.

"Yes, we're over by the Arby's!" he replied.

The fastest way to get where they were would have been to go right down the street, but that was no longer an easy task. To prevent rioters from breaching the fencing around the motor pool, police had come out the back of the building and were firing less-than-lethal projectiles at rioters who either got too close or were throwing objects. The path I had to take took me right in their line of fire. I had no other choice. I sprinted down the sidewalk and thankfully made it without getting hit.

I was rigged up to give my report to FOX News viewers. Waiting for the segment to start, what I believe to be a flashbang exploded not too far from where we were standing. Its force flung the body of the grenade right into my leg. "Oh shit!" I said instinctively, then immediately thought that I should probably not swear on live television if I got hit again with something.

During my report, I pointed out how I'd noticed three types of groups in the area. The first type were people who just wanted to protest peacefully. The second type were those who took part in the looting at the strip mall nearby. The third type were the looters and rioters whose principal aim was clashing with the police.

By the time of my segment, pretty much all the peaceful protesters were gone. Only rioters remained.

One of my favorite moments during my live report was at the end, when Laura thanked me and told me to stay safe, only for a flashbang to go off close by right as she said that. I truly felt like a foreign correspondent reporting from a riot as bombs fell and bullets flew.

My report went well, but the chaos was just ramping up. Rioters continued to violently engage with police officers, who were barely able to prevent the crowd from continuing to breach the perimeter. Rioters successfully tore down the fencing around the 3rd Precinct's motor pool.

Some in the crowd started talking about setting the building on fire with the officers still inside. Meanwhile, businesses near the 3rd Precinct that had survived Wednesday's violence were now being torched.

The mob had nearly surrounded the 3rd Precinct when we all noticed a convoy of police vehicles leaving the motor pool. Everyone quickly realized: **The 3rd Precinct was being abandoned.**

The sight of the Minneapolis Police Department evacuating invigorated the crowd to the point of frenzy. They pelted the convoy with rocks and other projectiles. Because of the mass of people, the police vehicles inched forward slowly as if caught in a rush-hour traffic jam. Its occupants were sitting ducks. Amid the shouts and screams, the air was punctuated with the sound of car windows being shattered and the thuds of projectiles bouncing off the armored personnel vehicles.

One such vehicle at the rear of the convoy pulled into the street. "Watch him on that truck!" one person screamed as an officer armed with a less-than-lethal weapon peeked out from the top and took aim. People began scattering.

I dashed towards a nearby parking lot. Whatever the officer shot made a loud snapping sound as it streaked past me. I had my phone in my hand recording everything I could. Not until I reviewed the video later did I realize several other shots barely missed me. I was fortunate to escape unscathed.

I slid down the small berm once I reached the parking lot while holding my phone above it to still capture video without exposing my head.

The last police vehicle pulled out of the motor pool, with officers deploying a large number of tear gas canisters and flashbangs to cover their retreat. This helped repel rioters trying to follow and attack the convoy. It stopped me in my tracks as well.

And just like that, the only police presence, as marginal as it was, was no more. The area was now in complete control of the rioters, like Saigon falling to the North Vietnamese or the Taliban taking Kabul.

As if with one thought, the crowd began breaking into the 3rd Police Precinct building to sack it and to set it on fire. Windows and doors were smashed. A mobile light tower was torn down and set ablaze in the motor pool, with people encouraging others to continue to make the conflagration bigger. The doors to the Precinct were eventually breached and people stormed in. Moments later, a rioter came out holding an MPD riot helmet high above his head. The crowd outside roared.

By the time I walked back to the front of the precinct, it was on fire. The crowd, overcome with the joy of victors, chanted, posed for selfies, and vowed to continue on to other police precincts.

"We didn't want to do this! [The police] made us do this!" one young man screamed. Fireworks were being lit and exploded over us in celebration. Across the street, the liquor and tobacco stores that had been looted throughout the day were now on fire.

I made my way back to my hotel, safely away from the chaos (I thought), thanks again to my new friend Jon. When I got there, I saw how the downtown area, which had been untouched earlier that day, was now starting to be targeted. I turned on the T.V. in my room just in time to see Minneapolis's Democratic mayor, Jacob Frey, host a late night/very early morning press conference. That's how I found out it was he who had given the order to evacuate the 3rd Precinct instead of providing reinforcements.

"What's the plan here?" one reporter asked bluntly. "What are we doing?"

"With regard to?" Frey replied after a pause.

"Oh, this city is screwed," I thought as I watched Discount Justin Trudeau bumble his way through the press conference. I called it a night.

MAY 29TH

When I woke up, I learned that the Minnesota National Guard and State Police had come out in force in the area around the 3rd Precinct. Taxis, Ubers, and Lyfts were nonexistent, so I walked the three miles back to where the chaos had played out the night before. Multiple buildings that survived Wednesday's anarchy were smoldering from the fires that had been set on Thursday. As I drew closer, the charred buildings and heavy smoke in the air made the area look like a complete disaster zone. The sunlight and quiet provided a stark contrast from the evening before, yet still gave off a creepy vibe.

A perimeter of police officers and National Guardsmen armed with M-16s had been set up so looters could no longer ransack the strip mall. A good idea, but several days too late.

Just like the day before, things were more-or-less calm during the day. Videos of locals helping clean up from the night before were going viral on social media.

"Too bad all that work is going to be undone tonight," I cynically, yet correctly, thought.

As time went on, more and more people began to show up to the perimeter. As the crowd grew, so did its aggressiveness. While some people were just trying to talk with the law enforcement line, asking if they agreed with what happened to Floyd or pleading with them to not use tear gas, others wanted to get right in their faces to scream and heckle obscenities.

"Y'all don't scare me!" one woman shouted right in the police officers' faces. "This is for us! This is for George Floyd."

The same woman shouted at the stoic police officers, "Y'all don't scare us! We will be here day in and day out, motherfuckers!" While I waited to see what would happen when the new 8:00 p.m. curfew rolled around, I saw on Twitter how the unrest in Minneapolis was beginning to spread around the country.

The CNN headquarters in Atlanta was under attack from their favorite "peaceful protesters." Ten minutes before curfew, the police and National Guardsmen took turns putting on their gas masks. A voice over a PA system informed the crowd it was time for them to head home or risk being in violation of the curfew.

That was all it took to transform protesters into rioters. They began to throw all the projectiles they had stockpiled nearby throughout the day. Almost immediately, the police line pulled back while firing tear gas and rubber bullets.

I wanted to get videos of the confrontation between the two sides clashing in the middle of the street. I found what I thought was a safe spot on the sidewalk. I was about halfway in between the two sides and recording the fighting when, out of nowhere, I felt a heavy smack in my stomach, like someone sucker punched me.

I had been shot with a rubber bullet.

My stomach felt like it was on fire. I keeled over holding my midsection. It hit me with such force—knocking the wind out of me hardly describes it—I didn't even think to utter a swear word, which I wouldn't have been able to do if I had.

"Oh shit," I thought, collecting my senses. *"I need to get out of here."*

Behind me on the sidewalk was a US Bank branch with a low green fence flanked by small bushes. I hopped the fence and fell on my back with my backpack breaking the fall. It hurt to get up. People who were watching everything unfold in the US Bank's parking lot rushed over to help me up.

"Do you need to go to the hospital?"

"Do you need water?"

I began to check myself. I wasn't coughing up any blood. While the area where I had been hit was in a lot of pain, it did not hurt to breathe.

"No, I'm good," I told the onlookers. I was still keeled over, just trying to focus on breathing. While it sucked to have gotten shot with a rubber bullet center mass, I was lucky I did not get hit in the head or the family jewels. After all, I had zero protective gear. My flak jacket and helmet were still at home in Virginia. I had not anticipated the full breakdown of social order when I flew to Los Angeles months before. Even the two-strap backpack I normally used to cover protests wasn't with me. Instead I used a 5.11 sling backpack intended for my commutes on the D.C. Metro, not long hours in the field.

I would later find out I had been shot with a 40mm Bullet Impact Projectile, which is a non-explosive version of the 40mm grenades the U.S. military uses. Non-explosive, but still the same size and very hard-hitting.

In the immediate aftermath of getting shot, my friend and colleague Kyle Hooten, who was livestreaming, rushed over to get me on camera. Ever the journalist, he asked how it felt to get shot with such a projectile.

"How does it feel?" I asked back in a sarcastic way. The pained look on my face answered the question better than any words.

It was about ten minutes later before I finally lifted my shirt to look at the wound. A large, almost perfect circle of skin was gone. It looked like an oversize piece of pepperoni was slapped onto me.

"Oh shit!" I said out loud. That got the attention of an Australian news crew. They shoved their camera up close to my wound. I gave a brief interview before telling them to move on since the rioters and police line were still engaging each other. I didn't want to miss anything. I patched myself up and pressed on, though at more of a distance. Meanwhile, the police line had completely pulled away from the area around the 3rd Precinct.

Once again, the area had fallen into the hands of the rioters, who continued their raucous and violent celebrating. Police used tear gas heavily to cover their withdrawal. The entire police line fell back down Lake Street to help the 5th Precinct, which itself was in danger of being overrun.

The rioters followed as best they could down Lake Street. Many broke off to loot and burn down other businesses that had survived the previous days. I was walking down the street where I once again found the

FOX News crew, which was fortunate since I was scheduled to be on Laura Ingraham's show again. I told them what had happened to me.

"You have to show it off during your hit, it'll make for good TV," the cameraman said.

I still had an hour before my appearance, and we continued to walk down the street, seeing the destruction spreading far down from the 3rd Precinct. We came upon a parking lot full of cars that were on fire. After I got set up to do the hit and we were waiting for the show to start, a set of agitators began to taunt us.

"Who are you with?" someone asked angrily.

"The news only showing up for the bad things!" another shouted as fires and looting were all around us.

We tried to ignore them by looking at our phones. I then made the mistake of looking up at them.

"Yeah, I know you can hear me!" one shouted.

They then positioned themselves to be right next to me and continued to berate us. I made a gamble to get rid of them. After all, I was planning on telling FOX News viewers the facts on the ground. The agitators weren't going to like what I was going to say,

"Look, I'm no fan of the cops either," I told them as I lifted up my shirt to show my future scar. "They shot me."

While it was not satisfactory to everyone in the group, with one telling me I was making it up, enough of them decided to back off and told the others to stop.

"Hey man, respect," one said to me as he shook my hand. They then left.

"Hmm, guess I should go topless more often," I joked to the crew.

I gritted my teeth while giving my report, complete with going "topless" for American viewers this time. Once it was over, I continued to walk with the crew but decided to take my bosses' advice and go to the hospital to ensure there was no internal damage.

I called a friend of my mom's in the voiceover community. He lived not too far from the action, and he provided me transportation to a downtown Minneapolis hospital. The CT scan came back all clear; it was just going to hurt for a while. Some of my friends gave me grief, saying I must have been happy to have gotten clout off of the incident, but I told them I would have gladly given that up since I missed most of the action at the

5th Precinct. I was unable to do my job that night because I had to make sure nothing serious had happened.

"I should have just not come to the hospital."

A police officer walked into my hospital room to ask what had happened to me. He heard I had been shot. I related what had happened; when I finished, he said he'd been told I had been shot with a real bullet.

"Oh," I said. "Yeah, as you can see, I wasn't shot like that. Sorry to have wasted your time."

While I was in the hospital, rioters launched an attack on the 5th Precinct, which was about three miles down Lake Street. Again, tear gas, flashbangs, and rubber bullets were used to push the crowds back, to little avail. A U.S. Post Office branch and a Wells Fargo branch were among the many establishments looted and set on fire.

I was not the only journalist to take fire. Photojournalist Linda Tirado was blinded in her left eye when hit with a rubber bullet near the 5th Precinct. The Press Freedom Tracker reported "dozens of journalists" had rubber bullets or pepper spray used on them during Friday and Saturday despite being clearly labeled as press.[1]

MAY 30TH

A brand-new day and America woke up in a "Ah shit, here we go again" mood. The pain from my wound was significantly less, only hurting if I moved my torso quickly. Thinking back to Marines who had suffered serious wounds during battle and continued to stay in the fight, a relatively minor injury was no excuse to get out of work. When I went downstairs to extend my stay, the front desk worker paused for a moment and asked, "Aren't you that reporter who got shot with something?"

"Uh, yeah, that was me," I replied, lifting my shirt to show the bandage to the shock of the desk worker and her colleague.

I headed back to the 5th Precinct. Once again, the situation was peaceful during the day. Activists gave speeches while protesters gathered in the intersection near the police building.

To pass the time, I toured the buildings damaged by rioters when they were unable to get close enough to the 5th Precinct. Large piles of garbage dotted the parking lot, mostly items that were left behind or didn't appeal to looters.

I found an office chair and exchanged stories with other reporters, comparing notes on what we had seen the past few days. The chairs seemed to have been saved from the inside of a burning building since the backs were partially melted.

A taco truck set up in a nearby parking lot. Protesters were not only *not* attacking it, they were waiting patiently in line to buy lunch—quite the contrast to the mood and actions after dark over the previous several nights.

As the 8:00 p.m. curfew neared, an alert was sent to all cell phones in the area, ordering people to go home. It seemed a toothless command. Protesters just sat down in the intersection as 8:00 p.m. came and went. Not a single police officer was in sight.

Ten minutes later, however, a column of officers quickly appeared, marching down the street in full riot gear. They clearly intended to enforce the curfew. Tear gas and flashbangs were deployed. Some protesters ran and scattered; others stayed and threw objects at the officers.

Trying to avoid a repeat of the previous day, I stayed behind the chain link fence that had been put up in front of the 5th Precinct. While I was filming the confrontations between the two sides, I saw movement on the building's roof.

"They're on the roof!" people in the crowd began to scream.

They didn't have to tell me twice. I, and much of the rest of the crowd, fled to safety. Flashbangs exploded all around. Rioters meanwhile began throwing the tear gas canisters back toward the police.

A sizable number of rioters refused to leave. Determined to fight, they had grabbed material from a nearby construction site to make roadblocks to halt the officers' advance. But enough law enforcement personnel were present to push many protesters back.

Naturally, the other members of the press were pushed back along with the rioters and protesters. An uneasy truce prevailed between the two groups. Things were mostly fine between us except for one instance where a man dressed in all black clothing and with a red cross taped on his shirt began to use a crowbar to chase away journalists and cameramen.

"Get going! Get outta here!" he shouted. "Fucking faggot piece of shit, go! You too, motherfucker, get out!"

If a photographer or reporter did not move fast enough, he would rush at them and raise the crowbar as if he was going to hit them. One cameraman was walking away and did not even notice the armed assailant. He had a piece of his equipment hit out of his hand by the crazed individual. I was able to record most of his threats and intimidation tactics while avoiding his attention. Part of me wanted to tell him to back off, but as I was by myself while not being at 100 percent and not knowing how many others would join him, I felt I had no choice but to walk away.

At this point, the crowd had been pushed into some residential areas in south Minneapolis. Despite their new environment, they continued in their attempts to build barricades to stop the advancing officers. One such makeshift barricade, made from construction material and dumpsters, was set on fire.

This time though, people who lived on the block confronted the crowd, and these residents were not happy.

"I'm trying to save people from getting shot!" one black protester shouted at a black resident. "People are losing their lives! I'm trying to save them!"

"You are? This is how you're trying to save them?" replied the resident as he pointed to the flaming barricade.

The protester shouted how the group had a "hospital" and the police had "shot it," as he banged his fists on one of the dumpsters.

"So this is the answer?" the resident replied, asking who was going to clean up the mess they were leaving behind.

Someone in the crowd shouted at him to "go to your fucking house, bro!"

Another black man across the street was yelling at the crowd to go home in more vulgar terms. He even shouted at me when I got too close to his lawn. Many of the initial group had left shortly after it was clear the police were going to finally enforce the curfew.

I heard a tip some activity was erupting back at the 3rd Precinct... Walking up Lake Street in the direction of the riots' Ground Zero, I saw multiple people standing outside of buildings and businesses, in some cases armed, to ward off anyone trying to loot or burn them.

One such building was the Division of Indian Work, an organization that provides programs for urban Native Americans. A man openly carrying a shotgun stood watch in front.

The organization had good reason to fear its building was not safe from rioters. A nearby building belonging to Migizi Communications, a nonprofit that provides media arts training to Native American youth, had been torched early Friday morning.[2]

During my walk along Lake Street, I was able to find the two components that made up the 40mm Bullet Impact Projectile with which I'd been shot. I was able to take home a twisted souvenir from the insanity of Minneapolis. It now sits on my desk on a trophy stand with a plaque that reads, "From: The Minnesota State Police (?) To: Julio Rosas."

The ad hoc citizens' security brigades were not just limited to businesses and organizations on Lake Street. Only a few blocks away from the 3rd Precinct, residents in nearby neighborhoods had set up roadblocks and stood guard by them, again with some being armed to varying degrees.

One woman at one of these barricades told me their neighborhood had a community meeting that morning to discuss what to do since the police were all but gone.

The best thing, they decided, was to put up roadblocks and only let people who live on the street inside their cordoned-off area. Just like those protecting their businesses on Lake Street, the neighborhood watches I met were made up of all races, all united in their desire to protect their homes and livelihoods when the local and state governments failed them in their most basic duties.

Lake Street and its side streets were oddly quiet compared to the fury of the previous nights. A few cars were still driving by, and some people were out on their porches, but overall the curfew was finally being adhered to.

Nearing the 3rd Precinct, I met a random live-streamer also walking towards the police station. We chatted as we walked but slowed our pace when we noticed people were gathered outside the burned building. Then a spotlight hit us. It was the police. They told us to go home or risk being arrested for violating the curfew order.

"We're press!" we shouted back.

The voice said it didn't matter and again told us to leave the area. We turned and walked away. By 1:00 a.m., it appeared as though the situation had calmed down. It took another hour for me to walk back to my hotel. I wondered if the unrest in the Twin Cities had finally ended.

MAY 31ST

Five days after the first eruptions rocked Minneapolis, the situation finally appeared to be under control, though far too late for many of the city's residents and business owners who had lost homes and livelihoods. Peaceful protests and marches continued, but the looting and rioting seemed to no longer be a problem.

One set of marchers near the U.S. Bank Stadium, home of the Minnesota Vikings, stayed out past curfew and went onto the highway to face a heavy contingent of officers. The police used flashbangs and tear gas to disperse some of the marchers, but a sizable number stayed in the area.

I met up with Kyle Hooten again, at which point we realized we were all being surrounded by police near a gas station. It was time to leave.

We went one direction that led us to a fence facing the highway, only to see a man scrambling over the fence towards us in a frenzy. Moments later, we heard the officers he was running from fire rubber bullets as the projectiles smacked into the fence.

We dashed for safety in a car wash, but knew this was not a good place to be cornered. Spying a camera crew for a local news station, we walked alongside them as they approached the officers who were closing in. Holding up our press credentials and pointing to the large video camera, we were allowed to leave. Kyle and I breathed a sigh of relief. The protesters weren't so lucky. The officers closed in and began making arrests for violating curfew.

Things were no longer out of control in the Twin Cities. Order was being restored, albeit slowly and after too much damage had been done. In other cities, such as Washington, D.C. and New York City to name two prominent examples, riots were just getting started.

I flew back to Los Angeles the next day, exhausted both physically and mentally. I didn't realize at the time this was a state I would be in constantly for most of the year.

At the airport, I tweeted a thought about what I had just seen and been through: "After personally seeing police completely abandon parts of the city and letting rioters/looters destroy private property and businesses, I never want to hear the phrase 'Nobody needs an AR-15' ever again. Law-abiding citizens should have access to those kinds of rifles."

There was a mild blowback to the tweet, often from people who weren't in Minneapolis, but it articulated a belief that I stand by to this day.

MINNEAPOLIS AFTERMATH

Minneapolis was a free-for-all. It was chaos, a harrowing example of the full breakdown of the social order. For several days—far too long—a state of nature prevailed in the worst sense. Regardless of what had happened with Derek Chauvin and George Floyd, in the incident's aftermath, the citizens of Minneapolis were betrayed by state and local government officials who left them to the predations of violent criminals and thieves.

Rioters got what they wanted because there were no police officers around for days. The cost of the short-term "abolishment" was immense. My belief in the tweet I sent solidified, as I would continue to document mayhem in different parts of the country.

Over $500 million of damage to at least 500 buildings in Minneapolis and St. Paul was incurred as rioters and looters had their way. Two people were killed. Sadly, many more would be killed in the crime wave Minneapolis experienced in the months that followed.[3]

Local authorities abandoned entire areas of Minneapolis. If you wanted to keep your store or home safe from the mob, you had better have a rifle or it wasn't going to end well for you.

What I want people to take away from my account of what I saw during my time in Minneapolis is that this was far from just a series of protests. Peaceful protests did occur, but there's a difference between protesting and rampaging.

Not everyone understood that most basic point, particularly many in the media.

Perhaps the greatest example of the media downplaying the riots was MSNBC anchor Ali Velshi's infamous words that are the title of this chapter. In Velshi's live report, he stated, "I want to be clear on how I characterize this. This is mostly a protest. It is not, generally speaking, unruly but fires have been started and this crowd is relishing that," Velshi added, as a building was engulfed in flames directly behind him. Velshi later addressed his comments, explaining he'd wanted "to emphasize that there had been and remained an overwhelming majority of the protesters who were peaceful." It was true there were peaceful demonstrators during the day, but by the time Velshi was reporting, the reality on the ground had changed, leaving many buildings that would be set on fire that night. I saw Velshi one more time before I left Minneapolis, and I still wish I had asked him why he downplayed the riots, because it became a pattern the mainstream media would use for the many riots that followed.

MSNBC anchor Craig Melvin tweeted what appeared to be the style guide for the far-left network's approach to the situation in Minneapolis.

Relaying official NBC News policy, he tweeted on the morning of May 28th: "This will guide our reporting in MN. 'While the situation on the ground in Minneapolis is fluid, and there has been violence, it is most accurate at this time to describe what is happening there as 'protests'— not riots."[4]

The city would go on to experience at least another two nights of riots after Melvin tweeted MSNBC's rule on denying the reality of the situation.

Even after the Twin Cities had been at the mercy of rioters and looters for multiple days, it did not stop some reporters from trying to get their snark in on Twitter.

At times this meant denying reality solely because they felt compelled to contradict President Trump.

On May 31, Trump tweeted, "Get tough Democrat Mayors and Governors. These people are ANARCHISTS. Call in our National Guard NOW. The World is watching and laughing at you and Sleepy Joe. Is this what America wants? NO!!!" President Trump tweeted on May 31st.

Enter Yamiche Alcindor, the White House reporter for PBS News who is widely known for her unobjective framing and observations.

"'These people are anarchists,' President Trump says without providing any evidence," she said on her timeline.[5]

2

CHAZ—The Radical Left's Failed Experiment in Democracy

I WAS BACK in Los Angeles for barely a day before I realized I had better return to the front lines. The anti-police riots in the Twin Cities were spreading to other parts of the country. In Seattle, protesters were openly waging battle with the city's police department at their East Precinct. The video footage being posted on Twitter convinced me I should head there to cover the action for Townhall.

The day before my flight, however, Seattle's Democratic mayor, Jenny Durkan, made a shocking decision. She ordered the Seattle Police Department (SPD) to abandon its East Precinct, located in the Capitol Hill area, in order to "de-escalate" the daily fights between officers and rioters. Several days later she would even tell CNN that CHAZ might come to resemble a "summer of love."

"Well shoot," I thought. *"Looks like I might have just wasted company money."* But something told me that the mayor's attempt to de-escalate the situation would hardly placate the mob. I decided to go anyway.

I arrived in Seattle on a Tuesday. After dropping my bags off at my hotel, I set straight out for the newly abandoned East Precinct. The scene was quiet. Cars passed by on the streets that had not been barricaded off.

About a dozen or so people wandered around inside the barricaded zone, the barricades consisting of fencing, garbage dumpsters (many overturned), bright orange traffic barriers, and concrete barriers on the sidewalk alongside the East Precinct. The buildings and barricades were covered in graffiti and plastered with signs declaring the area a "cop-free zone." The sign over the East Precinct had been altered; it now read "Seattle People Department."

Other signs took things further:

- "Capitol Hill Autonomous Zone"
- "You are now leaving the USA"
- "Welcome to Free Cap Hill"
- "You are now entering the Cap Hill Autonomous Zone"
- "You are now entering Free Capitol Hill"

The signs and graffiti were crude and improvised, but as the week wore on, the signage became more "official," more polished, more professionally designed. The attitude among the denizens in the streets became more entrenched that this several-block area would no longer have Seattle police officers patrolling the Capitol Hill neighborhood.

Soon, the "Capitol Hill Autonomous Zone"—or CHAZ—would become the moniker adopted by the protesters and their fans in the media for this novel experiment in local government.

With their newly established territory, the CHAZ occupiers set out to make the area a place for people to gather and bring about the change they saw was needed in Seattle.

Their first demand, and the organizing principle of CHAZ: Completely defunding the Seattle Police Department and removing any trace of their authority and presence. CHAZ would be self-governed and self-policed (whatever that meant). A further demand was that protesters be given immunity from prosecution. Since it's not illegal to protest peacefully, one assumes that demand meant immunity for anyone suspected of looting or rioting.

Supplies were donated by sympathetic locals and dropped off at The Cuff, one of Capitol Hill's gay nightclubs. I peeked my head inside. The floor was covered with piles of food, bottled water, and medical and personal-hygiene items. The club's owner said he was more than happy to use his now patron-free space for the cause. As I began to walk away, another person asked if I was helping to bring stuff over to a tent further inside the zone.

A light bulb went on in my head. I realized this could be my ticket inside the barricaded zone. My experience in Minneapolis had taught me how suspicious rioters were of *any* journalists in their midst, much less ones who wrote for conservative outlets and gave national interviews on FOX News. This could give me the cover I needed to infiltrate CHAZ.

"Uh sure, yeah," I replied, laughing to myself how a Marine with law-and-order sensibilities was being invited into the heart of the CHAZ rebellion. I got put on a working party in less than 20 minutes of being there. I spent the next 30 minutes lugging water, canned goods, and toiletries further inside the zone.

I stopped carrying supplies when I noticed workers with the Seattle Department of Transportation (SDOT) beginning to remove the overturned dumpsters that helped make up the makeshift barricades.

Stealing closer when I saw some of the self-appointed CHAZ leaders talking with SDOT, I heard the workers explain they had been instructed to remove most of the barricades, leaving behind only the bright orange roadblocks to prevent cars from driving through.

The occupiers were not happy with the news. They demanded SDOT leave *everything* behind because, they said, barricades were needed to help keep out any potential "white supremacists."

The SDOT workers tried to explain to the occupiers what they had been told to remove by their supervisors. The occupiers countered, saying they had agreed to something entirely different in their negotiations with the city. They argued back and forth for about 20 minutes. In the end the CHAZers won. The SDOT workers were only allowed to remove the concrete barriers on the sidewalk since they were not being used anyway. One day had barely passed, and the city had entirely given in to the demands of the occupiers.

Such interactions between the CHAZers and city officials and workers were common. The city would always choose the path of least resistance. Officials consistently appeased the increasingly radical occupiers instead of wielding the powers the city actually possessed to restore order, enforce laws, and protect people and their property.

One dynamic that particularly interested me was the relationship between the CHAZ occupiers, who did not appear to live in the neighborhood, and the residents and business owners who clearly did—folks who made regular rent/mortgage and property tax payments for the right to live in the Capitol Hill area. Certainly, I thought, they might expect the city to take steps to keep the area safe, secure, and open.

At the supply tent, one apartment resident whose building was right in the middle of CHAZ had come out to walk his dog and talk with his new "neighbors." He said the tenants were generally supportive of what was happening. They just wanted to know exactly what the end goal was for the new zone. Did the occupiers want an American version of Christiania, a commune in Copenhagen that began in 1971? He counseled that the occupiers needed to organize quickly or else the new zone could fall apart just as fast as it started.

One of the occupiers—a black man wearing a black tactical vest with an empty pistol holster on his leg—appeared understanding and even solicitous of the resident's concerns. He encouraged him to participate in a meeting scheduled to address such issues on Saturday, four days away.

Turns out that man was none other than Raz Simone. He would soon become known across the entire United States as the warlord of CHAZ.

Closer to evening, large numbers of people gathered at Cal Anderson Park to listen to speeches made by local anti-police and anti-Amazon activists. Among the speakers was the radically socialist Seattle city councilwoman Kshama Sawant.

A central thread running through these speeches was a demand that the Seattle Police Department be defunded. Speakers also called for the Seattle Police Officers Guild—the largest police labor union in the Northwest—to be removed from the King County Labor Council. (Within days, the Council did indeed vote to expel the Guild from its ranks. One Council official told the *Seattle Times* the Guild had "failed" at "actively working to dismantle racism in their institution and society at large.")

When the speeches ended, the crowd took to the streets. Ironically, they marched directly past a large mural urging people to stay home due to COVID-19.

The crowd headed downtown and had no trouble filing into the lobby of Seattle's City Hall. Turns out having a sitting city councilwoman as part of a protesting group has its perks, like using her key to get inside the building. The protesters packed the lobby, chanting for Mayor Durkan to resign.

The building's lone security guard stood off to the side, with no choice but to accept what was happening. No Seattle police officers responded to the protest. Luckily for City Hall, the protesters were not in the mood to smash windows or destroy property. They had their fun inside, shouting slogans and issuing demands, before marching back to CHAZ.

Back in the Autonomous Zone, a large projector screen had been put up. Social justice documentaries were shown, with the sound blaring over loudspeakers.

As in Minneapolis, the approach of nighttime would portend an evening of unrest. Raz Simone, already beginning to claim the mantel of leadership in CHAZ, would be at the center of the night's drama.

Videos showed an armed Simone, with his band of merry men, harassing a tagger for contributing to the growing amount of graffiti.

Someone live-streaming the confrontation was punched and attacked. Since Raz and his crew were the only ones armed in any significant way, any CHAZers interested in preventing wanton violence, vandalism, and graffiti could do nothing but yell at Raz to stop and leave. The new society was barely a day old, and it was already showing significant tensions.

More people gathered in CHAZ the following morning. The vibe was different from in the Twin Cities, where protesting quickly devolved into looting, destruction, and anarchy. In Seattle, there was an attempt, however feeble, to create something rather than merely destroy. In a land with no official police or government, Raz and his crew were attempting to fill the void. Not everyone was happy about that, and there were other claimants to power as well. But the fact that some had ambitions to do more than just loot and destroy was an interesting twist.

The topic on everyone's tongues was what to do with their newly carved out territory. The occupied blocks of Capitol Hill were slowly becoming the hub of left-wing activism the protesters were hoping for: Graffiti covered the neighborhood's buildings. Pro-Black Lives Matter signs and banners, posted on light poles and in windows, claimed the East Precinct was no longer a police station. It was now a community center.

The initial supply tent now anchored a growing "city" of tents, with people camping out in Cal Anderson Park. Granted, tent cities are par for the course for Seattle but *why* people decided to set up shop outside was significantly different. The CHAZ and Free Cap Hill signs were no longer made of cardboard or simply written on barriers; now such proclamations were being made into actual wooden and metal signs.

The dynamic inside CHAZ was fluid, depending on the time of day. There were several people who were generally seen as the leaders or spokespeople in the zone, but they were not present at all hours of the day and night. The situation was generally peaceful during the day. But that dynamic changed at night. Just as I saw in Minneapolis, the demographics changed from families and older people one would see during the day to younger people, often dressed in all black, at night.

Fights between people were not an uncommon sight. Moreover, CHAZ's self-appointed status as an "autonomous" zone was called into question after a fire was started in a dumpster next to a building that sat just outside CHAZ.

Despite claiming for itself the mantle of self-governance, CHAZ was in no way equipped to deal with a fire. Protesters called the Seattle Fire Department, then congratulated themselves for being "responsible" enough to call 911.

To their credit, Seattle firefighters came and put out the fire, to the applause of onlookers who said they loved the Fire Department, just not the police. It's worth noting that in addition to still being willing to use some of Seattle's taxpayer services, protesters also used porta-potties that were provided to CHAZ (and cleaned) by the city. Independence only goes so far, it seemed.

The dumpster fire was hardly the only crack to form in CHAZ's foundation. It became clear that its new version of street justice was not a suitable replacement for trained officers.

As the Seattle Fire Department was busy putting out the dumpster fire (and in the process extinguishing the idea of autonomous CHAZ), I saw a hostile crowd nearby surround a young man in a ski mask. They accused him of stealing a cell phone from another protester.

"You're not going nowhere," one person said to the visibly scared alleged thief. He denied stealing the phone, but the crowd was not buying it. After all, he initially had run away from them. If he were innocent, why run?

When it was noticed he did not have a cell phone on him, the mob speculated he could have just chucked it when he initially ran. One person in the crowd then turned the flashlight on his phone, shoved a baseball bat in the alleged thief's face, and said, "If you stole something, I'm gonna beat your ass."

The young man had two friends who were able to put themselves between him and the crowd, which allowed him to find a gap in the pack and slip out. He darted away, with some people once again giving chase, yelling "Thief, stop fucking running!" The alleged phone fanatic was able to disappear into the larger crowd of people. The phone he was accused of stealing, meanwhile, was discovered nearby.

While the young man was fortunate enough that the crowd did not assault him, as the weeks went by, in and around CHAZ, others were not so lucky. Some even ended up losing their lives.

The first days in CHAZ resembled seeing a newborn foal trying to stand up and walk on its legs, only to end up stumbling and falling down. But unlike the newborn who would eventually be able to trot and gallop to its heart's content, CHAZ never seemed to find its legs.

This was due to many factors—the lack of strong leadership being the main one. CHAZ was made up of a loose coalition of Black Lives Matter activists, community members, and Antifa/black bloc agitators, all of whom were in the zone at different times and different days, and many of whom had differing ideas of how things should be organized.

Sure, they all agreed that black lives matter, that the police department needed to be abolished—key word being _abolished_—and that they needed to hold the city blocks they were given. But determining how to achieve such goals was a major source of friction. Some organization was present for things like establishing guard shifts at the barricades and supply runs, but for the things that mattered to guarantee the zone's longevity, progress was not made.

This was made clear on the third morning when those gathered were broken up into small groups to discuss different actions that could be taken. Someone handed out a packet listing three options: Permanently taking over the East Precinct, moving the CHAZ to another location in the city to continue the movement, or dissolving the CHAZ so efforts could be redirected to "diverse action."

The language in the packet lamented that, despite CHAZ's formation coming about as a result of the police being ordered to abandon the East Precinct, they had not been resoundingly defeated in a "revolutionary action by dedicated communities."

The manifesto continued: "The lack of education around these ideas may lead to a lack of resolution and clarity necessary to maintain the movement or the co-optation or institutionalization of an autonomous movement by liberal capitalists, NGOs and politicians."

The packet added, "We must also recognize that many people currently working to build the CHAZ do not have experience with autonomous organizing. One of Occupy's major failures [a reference to the 2011 Occupy Wall Street protests] was excessively long and unproductive meetings, which eventually resulted in organizers taking power in order to accomplish things. We must figure out new ways to hear input from a group that does not involve massive 'general assemblies' every day."

Whoever created the packet clearly had the foresight and understanding of the problems CHAZ was already experiencing. Indeed, they were being proven correct at that moment, since it was being circulated at one of the numerous "excessively long and unproductive...'general assemblies'" it skewered.

But like many of the warnings given to the occupiers, the packet had zero effect. The massive meetings continued, often turning raucous but producing little in the way of answers. If any concrete progress was made at the meetings, I did not see its effects during the first week.

Another point of friction for the CHAZers seemed to materialize with the arrival of two SPD officers. Turns out the East Precinct was not totally abandoned. A small contingent of law enforcement personnel had remained inside the building. As the two officers made the short walk from the boundary of the CHAZ to the East Precinct's side entrance, their presence inside the "cop-free zone" was met with immediate hostility from many in the crowd.

One black man tried to act as an escort. He said he did not agree with them being there but he did not want anything to happen to the officers. A white woman on a bicycle tried blocking the officers' path, but the escort waved her off.

When they reached the precinct door, another black activist was able to get their attention and initiate a conversation. The escort, meanwhile, blocked the small stairwell to prevent anyone else from following. An argument broke out, with protesters complaining the officers' very presence violated everything CHAZers were trying to build.

"It doesn't matter how many cops are in here," said the man who'd escorted the officers safely. "We're not worried about police...we have the streets. We're not worried about police, bro!"

"I'm worried about police," one white man replied.

"You see I'm black, bro!" the escort retorted. "I'm not worried about police."

As if to reinforce his point about being worried about the cops' presence, the white man unbuttoned his shirt to show a wound from a crowd control munition with which he'd recently been hit.

The escort was unmoved. "I'm black! I'm BLACK!" he shouted. "I'm not scared of these police."

It was fascinating to see the Oppression Olympics playing out in real life and not on the internet. It seemed that while the white man "suffered" at the hands of SPD, his opinion did not matter as much because a black man was not concerned about the officers' presence at the moment. It was a complicated rock, paper, scissors, race game and woe unto you if you did not understand the hierarchy.

I turned my attention to the conversation the other activist was having with the police officers. The door to the precinct was open. More SPD officers could be seen inside.

"Our 911 response time has tripled [from] what it was," explained one officer about the effects of the numerous roadblocks in the area. "That's not acceptable. We have people being assaulted; we have people needing emergency response, and it's taking us 15 minutes-plus to get there."

When an activist said SPD needs to come down to the zone to just talk to the occupiers, the officer said they try to but are not met with people who want to talk.

As if on cue, people in the crowd began shouting for the officers to "get the fuck out of here!" The activist then went on to accuse SPD of "committing war crimes" against the protesters and rioters for utilizing tear gas to defend the East Precinct.

Once it became clear nothing was going to be resolved with the increasingly upset crowd, the officers went inside and shut the door.

It was not the only confrontational interaction these two officers had with the population. A since-deleted video posted to Twitter by local journalist Liz Pleasant showed one black man voicing his displeasure at the hostility directed towards the officers by a crowd unwilling to let them into the CHAZ.

"It's a precinct!" he implored them. "We need the police."

He was shouted down, and the officers were driven from the area.[6]

At one meeting of CHAZers, some black occupiers were berating their white counterparts for co-opting the larger BLM protests that originally started at the East Precinct. When a black occupier tried to defend these white protesters as allies, a black woman said he was not black, which drew audible gasps.

"Wow, she said I'm not black. What am I?" he responded. "Who are these people?"

Meanwhile, a Latino activist tried, unsuccessfully, to rally protesters to march on a grocery store outside of CHAZ. He claimed he had been subject to racial slurs about his mustache. People in the crowd did not believe him, saying it was a set up to make the CHAZ occupiers look violent.

The town halls were prone to becoming screaming matches, but they did have occasional moments when people were respectful and listened to a speaker. Generally, though, it was those with the means to be loudest who were heard.

———————————

As CHAZ continued to take shape, multiple tables and stands began to be set up along the sidewalk. There was a "No Cop Co-Op" with fruits, vegetables, and other perishables for people to take at no cost. "We do not accept cash or $ donations," said a sign above the co-op. "Kindness is our currency."

This of course begs questions about the logistics and money behind such an effort. Someone had to be footing the bill for the purchase and transport of grocery items, especially since they told people to not pay.

Other tents and tables sprung up for clothing donations and books. There was even a mental health station. Instead of calling it a mental health station or mental health help tent or Lucy's Psychiatric Help 5¢, they decided to call it a "Feelings Station." Make of that what you will.

The tent city in Cal Anderson Park was also expanding. What started out as a handful of tents became well over 30 in a few days, with a makeshift garden planted in the middle. There were about four plots for people to plant whatever they wanted. Because this was CHAZ, one segregated plot was designated only for certain people.

"This garden is for black and indigenous folks and their plant allies," a sign in front of the plot stated.

CHAZ was a few days old, and self-segregation for at least one thing was in style. But since this was Seattle, and the demographics of the city are whiter than a polar bear eating a Wonder Bread mayonnaise sandwich in the middle of a blizzard while watching Seinfeld, the garden plot was noticeably bare compared to the others.

By Friday, about four days since the formation of CHAZ, its denizens were starting to grow disillusioned with the name. Not only does CHAZ sound like it's the name of someone who is in a friend group with Chad, Brad, and Kyle, but CHAZers were beginning to realize just what they were asking for when they were demanding to be recognized as an autonomous zone.

Of course, the online mockery for their autonomous claim didn't help. After all, they were still utilizing the city's water, power, the aforementioned porta-potties, and even 911 emergency services in extreme circumstances.

They also realized that by declaring themselves to be independent of the United States, they were declaring themselves to be independent of the very rights that allowed them to protest in the first place. Thus, the "Capitol Hill Occupied Protest" was born and the CHAZ label was proverbially taken out back behind the co-op and shot.

Two black men claiming to be some of the leaders of the area gave an interview to KIRO 7 and said they did not know where the name "CHAZ" came from.[7]

"We're not sure if it were detractors or people trying to push a false narrative, but they definitely came in with that name, came in with signs, and they had nothing to do with our movement so far," one of the men, Maurice Cola, said.

"This is not an autonomous zone," he continued. "We're not trying to secede from the United States....We are expressing our legal application of these rights" to protest. He added that their preferred name for the area was CHOP, an acronym for "Capitol Hill Organized Protest."

All of which added up to another problem: What to do with all the CHAZ signs?

CHAZ/CHOP was barely a week old and already its occupants were rewriting history and taking down problematic tributes to their founding. The elaborate "Welcome to CHAZ" chalk drawing at the center of the zone's street intersection was changed to "Welcome to CHOP," though not all signs were easily accessible to be torn down and replaced.

The CHAZ "street sign" that was placed right in front of the East Precinct was bolted high on a telephone pole. To take it down, a ladder would be required. One person was in the process of taking the sign down, but an argument broke out at the base of the ladder. Some in the crowd were against removing it; others wanted him to continue.

To prevent the man from proceeding, some held on to the ladder and seemed to threaten to take it out from under him if he continued. Eventually, the man climbed down, but a struggle ensued over control of the ladder, which threatened to fall down onto the people below. An exasperated woman asked, to no avail, "Is anyone in charge?"

At this point, one man got hold of a megaphone to shame the crowd for arguing over a sign. He chastised them for becoming complacent as to why CHAZ/CHOP existed in the first place.

"It's been calm out here for a couple days and y'all arguing over a green metal sign? Shut the fuck up! Figure this shit out. Why are you out here?"

"Black lives matter!" a few people said.

"You see how slow the fuck that was?" the man asked. "Because y'all haven't been chanting for days. Y'all been singing. Y'all been dancing. Y'all been hanging out partying. Why are you here?"

"Black lives matter!" the crowd said with enthusiasm.

"That sign don't mean shit," he continued. "There's plenty of signs out here. Do we take down Pine [Street] because it doesn't go with [the movement]?...What the fuck y'all talking about?"

The sign stayed up overnight before being taken down Saturday afternoon, but not before someone crossed out the "Autonomous Zone."

Self-awareness was not a commodity much on display in the CHOP. A good example of this was when a white street preacher, who did not appear to have all mental cylinders firing, crashed one of the general assemblies on Saturday.

He climbed onto a stage while a pair of black women were talking and began shouting how they were in a "Christ zone!" He held a portable speaker that the occupiers tried wrestling from him. In a bizarre spectacle, he curled up into a ball as a mob of CHOPers attempted to remove him from the stage. During this comic struggle, they placed the preacher in a chokehold, a tactic commonly denounced by BLM activists.

This went on for almost five minutes. At one point, the woman at the microphone asked, "If there are any white people who have experience in security and maybe can talk to this gentleman?" In other words, she was effectively seeking a law enforcement officer to do what those who oversaw CHOP could not.

The irony did not stop there. Once occupiers finally got the man off the stage and ushered down the street, there were still confrontations between him and CHOPers. The street preacher claimed someone had taken his phone. During the screaming matches and near-fighting, one woman, who was only about half his size, tried to get onlookers to stand back as she went towards the scuffle.

"Mental health, we got this!" she declared, referring to being one of the ad-hoc social workers the zone had created in lieu of police officers.

"No, you don't got this!" two women screamed back, pointing to how the confrontation had been going on for well over twenty minutes.

The situation finally petered out, without the help of the social worker, when the street preacher seemed to run out of steam. But it highlighted that if this was the CHOP's response to adult men duking it out with each other, then there were probably going to be a lot more people who ended up getting hurt.

This reminded me of a flyer that had been handed out my first night on the scene. Produced by MPD150, an "independent, community-based initiative challenging the narrative that police exist to protect and serve," the flyer outlined what exactly a "cop-free" Seattle would look like.

Not surprisingly, it addressed the most common counterargument to abolishing police departments: Namely, how are you going to deal with criminals?

"Crime isn't random. Most of the time it happens when someone has been unable to meet their basic needs through other means. So to really 'fight crime,' we don't need more cops; we need more jobs, more educational opportunities, more arts programs, more community centers, more mental health resources, and more of a say in how our communities function. Sure, this is a long transition process, we may need a small specialized class of public servants whose job is to respond to violent crimes."

MPD150 conceded it would be unwise to just abolish a police department overnight.

To them, it would be a "gradual process of strategically relocating resources, funding, and responsibility away from the police and towards community-based models of safety, support, and prevention."

Instead of officers, "who very likely do not live in the neighborhoods they're patrolling, we want to create a space for more mental health service providers, social workers, victim/survivor advocates, religious leaders, neighbors and friends—all of the people who really make up the fabric of a community—to look out for one another."

Sounds great in theory, but like communism, MPD150's prescriptions don't take human nature into account. Not to say everything listed is not worth trying to pursue in tandem with keeping police officers, but the flyer argued against that idea.

As the CHAZ/CHOP circus continued, its dysfunction showed why police departments are found in virtually every city in any civilized country.

Later that afternoon tensions soared when a couple entered CHOP carrying giant American flags. Up to that point there were hardly any American flags seen inside the zone (I did see a United Nations flag being flown at one of the tents in the park).

One of the flag-wavers was Katie Daviscourt, a white local conservative activist. Max Hodges, a black Air Force veteran, accompanied her. I asked them if they were members of the Proud Boys, the right-wing group that rallies to fight Antifa on their home turf in Portland or Seattle. They said no. That was important to make clear since there were rumors about Proud Boys showing up to forcefully take back the area.

All they had were American flags; that's it. No Confederate flags or any symbol that I saw that could be viewed as white supremacy. The issue was that many in CHOP believed the American flag to be a symbol of white supremacy. Before reaching the borders of CHOP, the pair was heckled by people in the park.

"Fuck you!" one man said.

"Go home, you're drunk!" one woman said.

When Daviscourt and Hodges did reach the boundary of CHOP at E Pine Street and 10th Ave, CHOPers at the barricades heckled and booed them. Others stepped out to see why they were there in the first place. Eventually some of the white CHOPers were starting to yell at the crowd to not pay attention to the flag wavers because they just wanted attention.

That didn't sit well with everyone. A black CHOPer replied, "Don't tell black people what to do right now, how about that?"

"Fair, fair," one white man conceded, once again losing the game of rock, paper, scissors, race on behalf of white people.

Not satisfied with staying outside the zone, Daviscourt and Hodges entered CHOP. They walked through the area, waving their large American flags, trying to have a dialogue with people.

Some CHOPers ignored them, while others followed and hurled abuse at the pair. Daviscourt began speaking with a man wearing a Russian fur hat and sporting a Soviet star, who asked her why she would carry an American flag while claiming to care about black lives. Just then, a masked individual ran up and yanked the flagpole from Daviscourt's hands. A scuffle ensued, but CHOPers rallied to the defense of the thief, who was permitted to escape with the flag.

It was clear CHOP was no longer a safe place for Daviscourt and Hodges. They tried to double back and exit the zone, but an increasingly hostile mob was making that difficult. There were a few CHOPers who tried to protect them, but, it seemed, not enough. Someone threw his drink at them. Others began accusing the couple of being white supremacists, their only "evidence" to back up such an assertion being their American flags.

Amid the jostling, one CHOPer told Maurice Cola, "They're white supremacists; they don't deserve to talk."[8]

"That black guy is a white supremacist?" Cola asked.

"These two are," the CHOPer said as he pointed to Daviscourt and Hodges.

"That black guy that's holding the [American] flag is a white supremacist?" Cola asked again.

"He *with* a bunch of white supremacists. This is a Proud Boy, they're literal white supremacists," the CHOPer asserted.

Cola pushed back. "What they're doing here, holding the flag, doesn't cancel out what we're doing here. Everyone here is an American. I'm not suggesting their message matters. Their message *doesn't* matter."

Other protesters said that simply by walking into CHOP waving American flags, the pair was being "disrespectful." They should "get the fuck out."

Not that the crowd made it easy. Daviscourt and Hodges were accosted, heckled, and harassed at nearly every step of their retreat. But they did make it out safely.

I left CHOP on Sunday after spending almost a full week at the zone. It had not exploded into the orgy of violence and destruction I'd witnessed in Minneapolis, but tensions were rising. It was only a matter of time before the city's selective, hands-off approach would produce disastrous results.

Within a matter of weeks, my predictions came to pass. By the time city officials moved to finally put the CHOP experiment to an end, multiple crimes had been committed in the zone. These included "rape, assault, burglary, arson, and property destruction," according to Seattle police Chief Carmen Best.

The most serious crimes involved gunfire. At least four shootings occurred inside or adjacent to CHOP, resulting in the deaths of two black teenagers.[9]

Following public outcry over the shooting deaths, Mayor Durkan had no choice but to take back the area, which Seattle Police finally did during the early morning hours of July 1st.

Geoff Nelson, a local freelance videographer and photographer, gave me his eyewitness account on what he saw that morning (I was in New York City at the time).

What stuck out to Nelson most was how quickly SPD was able to enter CHAZ/CHOP and push everyone out of the area so crews could clean up the mess that had been left behind:

My phone rang at 5:00 a.m. on July 1, 2020. My network client on the other end telling me that Seattle PD was massing near

Broadway and Pike St. The thought was they might be moving in on CHAZ. Many of us in Seattle media had a feeling today was the day. The Capitol Hill neighborhood where these few blocks had been taken over was fed up-the violence had been increasing, and everyone was looking to Mayor Durkan and SPD to close it down and get it cleaned up.

As I got dressed, got downstairs, and got my gear sorted in my truck, I had a nervous sense about how this might end up. The security forces inside of CHAZ were known to be armed and they had threatened with violence any outsiders that had ideas of disrupting their newly held territory. Equipped with a ballistic vest and gas mask, I met my network client's producer and correspondent near downtown, where we made a quick plan of action with our three-man security team. We traveled together to just outside the radius of CHAZ and got setup inside a business that our security team was friendly with. We were able to park inside a secure, gated area-making that our base of operations.

We talked over a safety plan and headed south on 12th Ave towards E. Olive St. Instantly the sound of an SPD speaker ordering people off the streets could be heard. We followed that announcement down E. Olive to 11th Ave and the border of Cal Anderson Park. SPD was clearing that side of the park and marching south down Olive in full riot gear. You could tell they were on a mission. Today would be different than other days.

We waited for SPD to get about a hundred feet ahead of us and we fell in behind them. With my camera on my shoulder, and constantly rolling, we trolled down 11th toward E. Pine St, the epicenter of CHAZ. SPD was everywhere, working every corner of the four-block area, in tandem with Seattle Dept. of Transportation. What few stragglers that remained, SPD hustled them out of the area while SDOT began cleaning up. And there was a lot to be cleaned up.

We ended up finding the most activity, and most illustrative video that would tell today's story, at the intersection of E. Pine and 11th. The front door of the SPD East Precinct faced this corner. Still hanging near that entrance was the huge banner put up in the early days after Mayor Durkan had surrendered the precinct—it read,

'THIS SPACE IS NOW PROPERTY OF THE SEATTLE PEO-PLE.' That banner and all the other signs and installations would disappear in a matter of hours.

My team and I worked to document and shoot the events there as quickly as we could. SDOT had moved in with trucks and small cranes to remove the concrete barriers that they had installed as a sort of defensive wall against cars speeding through the area, which was always covered in humanity. Giant piles of trash were being created as the crews went through the area. Signs that had graffiti or artwork on them were put on trucks and saved, probably as a directive from the Mayor's office or SPD, in an attempted sign of good will. Makeshift shelters were ripped apart, portable tents were taken down, furniture was removed. SPD and SDOT workers faced zero resistance as they worked, anyone and everyone that had been living in CHAZ, or at least inhabiting the streets there, had vanished.

After spending 20 minutes or so documenting the cleanup events in the intersection of E. Pine and 11th, we pulled off a quick live shot for the network, providing some of the first up close and personal television images of the end of CHAZ for a national audience. Shortly following that live report, SPD told us to get out and up E. Pine one block, behind a police barrier. From that vantage point on a hill, we could see down E. Pine towards Broadway, through the heart of the once nationally famous 'autonomous zone.' CHAZ was quickly becoming a thing of the past.

We spent the rest of the day watching the clean-up, inching closer to the intersection where we began our early morning. SDOT crews worked with amazing speed. By noon, 11th was almost clear except for the piles of trash that would later be taken care of with large dumpsters. The banners covering the front of the East Precinct came down. A man on a ladder worked on the Seattle Police Department sign with a high-pressure water hose, erasing the graffiti that had temporarily changed the name to the Seattle 'People's' Department.

The street sign that read, 'Welcome to Capitol Hill Autonomous Zone,' and which was mounted on a telephone pole outside the precinct, was carefully removed and thrown in a truck.

A large, clenched fist, symbolizing Black Lives Matter, was also removed. The SDOT worker in a cherry picker lift handled both signs with some reverence, probably trying to follow orders as best he could to preserve the symbols that represented a now closed chapter in Seattle city history.

The sickest irony of CHAZ/CHOP was how it was created to be a "safe place" for people of color, yet the people who died in and around the cop-free zone were black.

Obviously, people of color die in areas where police operate, but with the expulsion of police in that portion of Capitol Hill, it all but guaranteed the harm or death of minorities.

"I think the CHAZ/CHOP experience says it all," Mike Solan told me. Solan is president of the Seattle Police Officers Guild, the police union that had been ejected from the King County Labor Council. "Look who the victims of violent crime were when there were no police around. The biggest proponent of law enforcement are communities that are plagued by crime."

Solan told me his main concerns during the height of the riots at the East Precinct were the assaults on SPD officers and the rhetoric from the Seattle City Council.

"It was quite clear we weren't getting support from elected officials to hold the line every night right in front of the East Precinct, and I think ultimately the city felt the pressure," Solan said. "I think the mayor's office caved."

Solan described SPD officers' "utter disappointment" when the order came down to leave the East Precinct, adding they were concerned the building was going to be broken into and burned down as soon as officers left the neighborhood.

Their reaction to Durkan's "summer of love" remark? "Bewilderment." He added that not getting "the backing of our elected officers, the injuries to officers who were ordered to hold the line and protect that precinct and just the fact that CHAZ...became an actual reality" only increased this feeling among the SPD rank and file.

In the aftermath of the city's CHAZ/CHOP fiasco and officials' failure to support the city's police department, it should come as no surprise that scores of SPD officers have left the force for new or better opportunities.[10]

"I think there's only so much a human being can take," Solan told me. "The public needs to understand that cops are just human beings. We have personalities; we have feelings. When you're besmirched, when you're ridiculed and you're not supported by your elected officials day in and day out, when I haven't heard anybody from the city council show concern for the injuries the officers are being afflicted with, I can understand that sentiment. Do I think it's widespread? I think people are frustrated, and everybody is different. Everybody has their breaking point."

It seems as if Mayor Durkan recognized that point as well. In December, she announced she would not run for reelection.

SEATTLE AFTERMATH

If CHAZ/CHOP produced anything, it was an abundance of irony. The best example came courtesy of Seattle's civic leaders—Mayor Durkan in particular—who placated the demands of a mob despite the fact that the mob would happily abolish the city's governmental structure if it could.

Durkan sang high praises for CHAZ/CHOP and what it stood for in the early days. Yet everyone in the zone seemed to hate her. Not only did CHAZ marchers flood City Hall and demand Durkan resign, inside the zone I saw many tables collecting signatures for her recall.

Despite its many problems—the squalor, the violence, the lawlessness—CHAZ got glowing reviews from big news publications.

USA Today, for instance, compared it to a "mini-Burning Man festival, complete with its own corps of volunteer street cleaners and medics, as well as dreadlocked white girls blowing soap bubbles and taking selfies in front of paintings of men and women killed by Seattle police."[11]

Politico's over-the-top contribution was titled, "Don't Listen to Fox. Here's What's Really Going On in Seattle's Protest Zone," complete with its own Burning Man comparison:

> What's going on in these four blocks that shook the world is indeed an occupation, but it looks nothing like the conquista touted on Fox. It's also the 'block party' that Mayor Jenny Durkan has compared it to, to gleeful jeers from Fox commentators. And it's other things as well—a protean, issue-focused but conceptually sprawling formative community, at once silly and serious, spontaneous and disciplined. Over the course of two evenings and an

afternoon in the zone (plus a night observing a police/protest show-down there the week before), it seemed by turns like a commune (as in Paris 1871), an anarcho-syndicalist and small-L libertarian dream, a '60s-style teach-in, a street fair and street market, a cam-pout and weekend party, a poetry slam and pilgrimage, a school service day, a mass healing circle, a humbler urban version of Burn-ing Man, and of course a protest rally.[12]

Rolling Stone published a similar article ("Seattle's Autonomous Zone Is Not What You've Been Told") that gives a window into the mainstream media's obsession with FOX News more than its devotion to reporting facts.

"Acolytes of Fox News detect a raging cauldron of antifa-led insurrec-tion," wrote reporter Rosette Royale. "But step inside the Jersey barriers that block off numerous streets, and you'll soon realize something else: It's a peaceful realm where people build nearly everything on the fly, as they strive to create a world where the notion that black lives matter shifts from being a slogan to an ever-present reality."[13]

The problem for *Politico*, *Rolling Stone*, and others, is that CHAZ *was* exactly like what FOX News was telling its viewers. Chico Marx famous-ly asked, "Who ya gonna believe, me or your own eyes?" Thanks to their sham reporting on the events in Seattle, Minneapolis, and elsewhere, the mainstream media ended up with less credibility as serious news organi-zations than Chico, Harpo, and Groucho.

Several weeks into the CHAZ/CHOP experiment, the ludicrous asser-tions of its media cheerleaders had been exposed. The violence and may-hem and general lawlessness could no longer be ignored.

There are those who would insist "the real CHAZ/CHOP was never given a chance,"[14] but my time in that South Park hippie-episode-come-to-life showed me it could only end in failure.

If anything good could be said to have come from the whole affair, it was the hilarious names the Twitterverse and others came up with to mock Seattle's failed experiment at building a new society: Soyviet Union, Wokadishu, Antifastan, Soymolia, Veganzuela, Woko Haram, Soyattle, and Discount Petoria.

3

The "Federal Invasion" of Portland

IF IT'S a day ending in "Y," there's a good chance protests are raging in Portland, Oregon. Portland had earned a reputation for senseless urban confrontation long before George Floyd's death sparked unrest in other American cities.

In the aftermath of Floyd's death, the Antifa and progressive blocs for which the city is known kicked their agitation up a notch. Even when the violence that sprang from Black Lives Matter finally began to die down in most cities, Portland's radicals kept the party going.

I had been to the City of Roses before, in 2019, to cover a confrontation between Antifa and the Proud Boys. I saw firsthand how much this supposedly beautiful city was, for lack of a better term, a dump. When I returned in 2020, I was surprised by the degree to which its post-Floyd rioters had made the city even worse.

Like the Kool-Aid man bursting through a wall, the riots in Portland broke through the news cycle and became *the* national story of urban unrest during the month of July. The nightly battles at the Mark O. Hatfield United States Courthouse were the center ring attraction in Portland's circus of protests and riots.

After Seattle, I spent two weeks away from frontline reporting for my annual training with the Marine Reserves. When I returned, I headed straight for Portland.

Throughout June, the city's Antifa and black bloc groups had focused mainly on the Portland Police Bureau's precincts and the county's Justice Center. And when CHAZ/CHOP became a media cause célèbre three hours north in Seattle, Portlanders tried their best to create their own police-free autonomous zone. They failed, however, in no small part because they made the mistake of doing so right outside the apartment complex where the city's Democratic mayor, Ted Wheeler, lived. (He would eventually move after rioters tried setting the building on fire.)

As June came to a close, Portland's rioters set their sights on the Hatfield federal courthouse.

That development changed everything.

Up to that point, the riots in Minneapolis, Seattle, and other cities had been local affairs. They were of national interest, certainly, and were covered heavily by national and even international news media. They centered on local neighborhoods and local businesses. They were the responsibilities of state and local authorities to handle. (How or even whether they handled them was a different matter.)

An attack on the federal courthouse in Portland turned a decidedly local affair into one that concerned the federal government. And who sat atop the Executive Branch of the federal government? President Donald J. Trump.

Trump wasn't going to follow the lead of officials in Minneapolis and Seattle, who abandoned and conceded police precincts to rioters intent on pillage and destruction.

With the courthouse squarely in Antifa's crosshairs, President Trump signed an order to reinforce the Federal Protective Service (FPS) officers who were already there—a perfectly sensible move to safeguard a federal building from angry mobs.

That's not the way Antifa, national Democrats, and even many in the media saw it. They denounced the president's action as an "invasion" of federal officers. Of course, such an "invasion" never would have happened had the rioters left the courthouse alone. But by poking the bear, they invited the federal government's involvement in Portland.

When I arrived in Portland, the action at the courthouse was still going strong. There was no law enforcement outside the building, but that did not stop the rioters from attempting to break into the fencing perimeter and throwing large-grade fireworks of the sort used by professionals at Fourth of July celebrations.

The FPS gave the crowd multiple warnings to stop attacking the courthouse and setting fires. To no surprise, these were ignored. After numerous people had breached the perimeter and continued tearing down the fence, federal officers came out in force with flashbangs and tear gas. Pepper balls were fired. The feds even had a tear gas equivalent of a fog machine to help force people away from the building. Officers carrying heavy-duty fire hoses shouted, "Make a hole!" so they could douse the flames.

The feds' tactics worked...sort of. Portland's highly experienced Antifa and BLM groups had long turned rioting into an art form. They were more than prepared to counter flashbangs, tear gas, and pepper balls. They had shields, leaf blowers, gas masks, and umbrellas to protect themselves while making their retreat.

A cat-and-mouse game ensued that would play out over and over. Federal officers would come out beyond the fencing, flanking the rioters and trying to arrest any individuals they could catch (most easily ran away). As officers would drop back to the courthouse, rioters followed close behind. On and on it went for hours, until the rioters' ranks thinned out as night gave way to morning.

While the violence was deadly serious, it was not without its comic moments. The Department of Justice charged 18-year-old Gabriel Agard-Berryhill with throwing an explosive device that set the main entrance of the courthouse on fire on July 28th. Hilariously, federal investigators were able to connect Agard-Berryhill with the bombing through an online product review made by his grandmother about the vest he wore to the nightly riots.[15]

One false narrative to come out of the Portland riots held that the federal officers were an unidentified, Gestapo-like invasion force sent to suppress the peaceful gatherings with tear gas and "kidnapping" protesters in unmarked vans.

Nothing could have been further from the truth. In my time there, I saw the Antifa/Black Bloc groups routinely make the first moves in their altercations with federal officers. Night after night I heard the FPS give multiple warnings, only for them to be ignored. Only then did the officers finally come out to put a stop to their vandalism and attacks.

As the officers did come out, one could clearly see the agencies they represented—U.S. Marshals, Customs and Border Protection, or Department of Homeland Security—from the patches on their uniforms.

Despite ample photographic evidence to the contrary, the false narrative about the feds as instigators circulated throughout media accounts:

- "'Secret police force': Feds reportedly pull Portland protesters into unmarked vehicles, stirring outrage"—*USA Today*[16]
- "Mysterious arrest video with unidentified police raises questions"—CNN[17]
- "The unmarked federal agents arresting people in Portland, explained"—*Vox*[18]
- "Unidentified Federal Agents Are Detaining Protesters in Portland"—*New York Magazine*[19]

Not surprisingly this line of argument was a staple in the talking points recycled by Democratic politicians:

- "Unidentified stormtroopers. Unmarked cars. Kidnapping protesters and causing severe injuries in response to graffiti. These are not the actions of a democratic republic. [DHS's] actions in Portland undermine its mission. Trump [and] his stormtroopers must be stopped. First Amendment speech should never be met with one-sided violence from federal agents acting as Trump's secret police, especially when unidentified. This is disgraceful behavior we would expect from a banana republic—not the government of the United States."—Speaker of the House Nancy Pelosi.[20]
- "A peaceful protester in Portland was shot in the head by one of Donald Trump's secret police. Now Trump and Chad Wolf are weaponizing the DHS as their own occupying army to provoke violence on the streets of my hometown because they think it plays well with right-wing media."—Oregon Senator Ron Wyden[21]
- "We didn't ask for these troops in our cities. We don't want these troops in our cities."—Portland Mayor Ted Wheeler[22]
- "Nobody is condoning violence against anyone, by anyone. This hearing is titled, 'The Right of the People Peaceably to Assemble: Protecting Speech by Stopping Anarchist Violence.' But the hearing we should be having is one called 'The Right of the People Peaceably to Assemble, Without Being Beaten Up by Unidentifiable Federal Agents.' That would address an actual problem lawful protesters are facing and the rest of us are seeing in this country."—Hawaii Senator Mazie Hirono[23]

New York Times Op-Ed Columnist Nicholas Kristof was among the worst offenders pushing the false narrative that the federal officers were attacking peaceful protesters without provocation, tweeting: "I think how sad Mark Hatfield, a deeply ethical Oregon senator who opposed the Vietnam War, would be to see the US courthouse named for him 'defended' by federal troops who beat and tear gas peaceful protesters, even kidnap people off the street. Hatfield would condemn this."[24]

In response to a tweet from former Acting Director of the United States National Intelligence Richard Grenell about how terrible the city's leadership was, Kristof wrote, "Rick, come to beautiful Portland, and you'll find that the 'city in flames' narrative is nonsense. There are a couple of blocks in downtown that are in tumult each night, though, partly because the Trump administration dispatched troops to inflame the situation for its benefit." (Kristof, Twitter 2020)

Kristof was so committed to the false narrative, he even devoted one of his *New York Times* columns to the topic. Snidely titled, "Help Me Find Trump's 'Anarchists' in Portland," the column sarcastically asks if the street medics and musicians at the protests he attended were the "anarchists" the president had criticized. "Sure there are anarchists and antifa activists in the Portland protests, just as there are radiologists and electricians, lawyers and mechanics. Report on the ground here and any single narrative feels too simplistic. The protesters aren't all peaceful, nor are they primarily violent. They're a complicated weave, differing by time of day."

During a press conference in Washington, D.C., on August 6th, I asked Acting Customs and Border Protect Commissioner Mark Morgan about the smears that Democrats and some in the mainstream media were making against the officers.

"It's outrageous at this point. In the beginning, I'll give them the benefit of the doubt. I tried to give them the benefit of the doubt," Morgan said. "We've bent over backward. DHS, the Secretary, the Deputy Secretary, both of them have now testified. We've gone on the Hill, all of us."

Morgan continued, "We've given an exorbitant amount of evidence that absolutely puts that false narrative to bed. The individuals that are still saying that, they simply are lying. They simply don't want to hear the truth. I've been a career law enforcement guy for 30 years; I've never seen it this bad."[25]

I'll note that the only time I saw police using unmarked vans to arrest people was when they tried to sneak up on rioters throwing projectiles at officers stationed behind the courthouse fence (unsuccessfully, as it turned out; the culprits all ran away before the officers could spring from the vans). By and large, however, there was nothing secret about the presence of federal officers defending a federal government building.

Another ludicrous argument many Democrats and their media allies pushed was that if Trump were to remove the extra federal reinforcements, then the unrest would cease since rioters would no longer need to defend their city from an "invading force." That sidesteps the fact that the reinforcements were only sent by President Trump *after* the courthouse had come under attack in the first place.

In the end, the federal officers did withdraw, part of an agreement between the Trump administration and Oregon officials. The state's Democratic governor, Kate Brown, announced in late July that the Oregon State Police (OPS) would be taking over security for the area outside the federal courthouse.

The situation at the courthouse did become peaceful for a few nights afterwards. Still, riots continued in other areas, notably at various Portland Police Bureau (PPB) stations throughout the city that had been targets of rioters' attacks prior to the celebrated assaults on the Hatfield Courthouse.

It's worth noting that the State Police stopped providing security for the courthouse not long after assuming that responsibility. When it became clear that many of those arrested in Portland's riots were not going to be tried by Mike Schmidt, the district attorney for Multnomah County, the state police rank-and-file rebelled. In a thinly veiled statement, an OSP spokesman said, "At this time we are inclined to move those resources back to counties where prosecution of criminal conduct is still a priority."

Fortunately for the situation at the courthouse, the rioters had largely moved on at this point to other targets throughout Portland. In one instance, rioters attacked two elderly women outside PPB's East Precinct. One woman had paint dumped on her head. The other woman, who was using a walker and holding a BLM sign, was stopped from putting out a fire with a fire extinguisher.[26]

Perhaps the most disturbing example of general lawlessness in the city came on August 16th. Kalen D'Almeida, an independent journalist and co-founder of *Scriberr News*, captured video of a BLM-aligned mob dragging a driver from a pickup truck. The driver, later identified as Adam Haner, was attacked seemingly for no reason. D'Almeida's video showed a man in a ballistic vest come at Haner from behind and viciously kick him in the face, knocking him unconscious.[27] The attacker was later identified as Marquise Love, a 25-year-old local BLM activist with a lengthy criminal record.[28]

"So they're surrounding [Haner], and they're yelling at him, doing all types of stuff. There was Marquise Love and he was just aggressive and violent," Kalen recounted to me. "This group was just beating up...It started with one guy and then another person, and then a trans person. This chick full on tackled Adam Haner's girlfriend...Nobody was doing anything to stop [Love]."

"Haner is lying in the street. [The crowd] drag him over near his truck, and they're pouring water on his face and they don't really know what to do; he's not really responsive. You could hear one guy claiming responsibility...screaming 'BLM! BLM!'—claiming responsibility for what was going on," Kalen said.

When it was finally time for me to leave Portland, my ears were hurting from the flashbangs and fireworks exploding for hours on end throughout the city.

The ringing I had been hearing, which began in Minneapolis, had become a bit louder. I had brought a pair of earplugs with me, but somehow lost them before putting them to use. While packing for my escape from Portland, what did I find tucked snuggly in the pocket of a pair of pants? My "lost" earplugs.

"Son of a..."

JANUARY 2021

In Portland, any excuse is a good excuse to riot. I was back in the Rose City five months after the summer's rioting at the Hatfield Courthouse. This time, I was on hand to document the violence that was sure to come after local radical groups called for "direct action" to coincide with President-elect Joe Biden's upcoming inauguration.

Make no mistake: They weren't planning to celebrate Biden's taking the oath of office as president.

Antifa's message to Biden was simple: We're real and we hate you.

One banner they carried during their daytime march read: "WE DON'T WANT BIDEN—WE WANT REVENGE!"

The first march of the day started at Revolution Hall. The crowd of about 150 black-clad marchers became angry after the Portland Police Bureau told the group over a loudspeaker not to march in the street. The road was supposed to be open for cars. That was the worst possible thing the police could have said. Immediately, the crowd flooded the streets.

One woman with a megaphone admonished those in the crowd who just wanted to fight with cops. She said they ignored how their actions were putting the lives of the BIPOC marchers in danger.

A transgender black woman then yelled at the marchers who were walking away while the other person was speaking. "That is disrespectful!" she yelled. "That is fucking rude!" Those walking away screamed back they didn't care.

After wandering for several blocks, the crowd found itself in front of the offices of the Democratic Party of Oregon. It did not take long before some in the group spray painted vulgarities about Biden and their typical slogans on the building's exterior.

"Fuck Joe Biden"

"ACAB"

"Fuck PPB"

Others brought over umbrellas to block police and the media from seeing or filming the wanton vandalism. I stood right behind the line of umbrellas to discreetly film their actions.

Then some Antifa actors tried to take the destruction to the next level. They began smashing the building's windows and front door using metal rods, tools, and batons. A few of them, however, had a difficult time mustering the strength to actually cause damage. One of them punched a window, but only succeeded in hurting his hand. Another "comrade" walked up with a baton and hit the same window, but the window stood firm. The pair gave up on that window but were able to break the one next to it (and only because someone else had broken it in another spot).

Meanwhile, their associates started pulling the garbage dumpsters into the street and setting their contents on fire.

Police in an SUV that had been following the crowd announced over their loudspeaker that arrests were going to be made for damaged property. This was enough to send much of the crowd scattering. Police arrested eight individuals in connection with the attack on the Democratic headquarters.

The next Antifa target was the Immigration Customs and Enforcement (ICE) station in the city's south waterfront district. Aside from the PPB precincts and the federal and county courthouses, the ICE facility was a popular spot for protest. Antifa marched to the location after gathering at a nearby park. The crowd, again about 150 strong, chanted "Fuck Joe Biden!" and painted graffiti on the facility's walls.

Just like at the Hatfield Courthouse during the summer, the FPS gave multiple warnings to the crowd to stop trespassing on federal property. While their actions were criminal, the January violence was tame compared to what I saw at the courthouse in August.

After declaring it to be an unlawful assembly, federal officers came out to disperse the crowd with the usual array of flashbangs, rubber bullets, tear gas, and pepper balls. Because this crowd was much smaller than during the courthouse siege, the Antifa gathering scattered much more quickly, though they regrouped down the street.

The cat-and-mouse game started up once again. This time, however, Portland police showed up to help the feds. PPB officers in riot gear came to take control of the situation outside and allow the federal officers to go back inside the ICE building. Meanwhile, Antifa rioters set an American flag on fire. A Biden 2020 flag was to add to the pyre.

"Fuck Joe Biden!" they chanted as the flags burned.

Unlike the federal courthouse, the ICE station was located right next to apartment buildings. Residents appeared on their balconies, angry not at the officers but at the Antifa agitators. This was clearly not the first time Antifa had disrupted their sleep.

One black resident yelled, encouraging the officers to arrest everyone. He yelled at the crowd as well, hurling a "Your mom" joking insult at an Antifa heckler. Another man opened his balcony door, shouted, "GO THE FUCK HOME!" at the top of his lungs, and walked back inside.

Tim, the owner of a nearby business, stood outside his building to ward off any person thinking of breaking any more of his windows. Still, he was relatively sanguine about the challenge his business was facing at the moment.

"It's not the protests that bothers any of us down here," he told me. "It's the late nights [that require me] to be down here. Sometimes it's 2 or

3 o'clock in the morning then I got to come back down again the next day. That's the only problem; I lose sleep. I've replaced windows; I replaced a window this morning."

When I asked Tim* if he thought the city had done enough to clamp down on the destructive behavior, he responded, "Not even close." He explained, "I think it got way out of hand, quickly. I'm not trying to be pro-left, pro-right....It gets to the point when it's beyond protesting, and it gets violent. [It's the] destroying businesses or hurting people that I have a problem with."

Tim told me he did not believe the riots were going to calm down any time soon now that Biden was in office. The local Antifa groups were just looking for any excuse to riot. He also noted the apartment complex that was closest to the ICE station was for low-income residents.

PORTLAND AFTERMATH

Natives of the Pacific Northwest and older folks often tell me that Portland used to be such a beautiful city. While the mountain scenery was certainly nice to look at, the actual city itself only serves to cement my dislike for cities in general. I certainly believe Portland, along with places like Seattle, are doomed to be stuck in their hamster wheel of destruction.

Even though they are not actually overflowing with rioters, they enjoy the support of those who do not take to the streets to cause unnecessary mayhem themselves. Mayor Wheeler did not even call out Antifa by name until a press conference he held after a riot occurred on New Year's Eve in 2020, long after the city had experienced nightly riots.[29] For the people who say Portland used to be a great city to live in, I'll have to take their word for it.

---

*Real name has not been used.

4

"Fiery But Mostly Peaceful"

AUGUST 23, 2020

Just as when I saw the George Floyd video posted on Twitter back in May, I knew the situation in Kenosha, Wisconsin, would devolve into chaos after a video on social media showed a white Kenosha policeman shoot Jacob Blake, a black man, in the back seven times.

And just as in the other situations, no one knew the full story of what led up to the shooting. But much like other police-involved shootings, it did not matter. The only thing that mattered was a white officer shot a black man.

What initially struck me was that this was not the first time I had heard of little-known Kenosha. My first duty station in the reserves was Marine Air Control Group 48 at Naval Station Great Lakes in Illinois. The sergeants in my section lived in Kenosha, about 30 minutes away, and even hosted a cookout during one annual training. Kenosha was not a major American city like Minneapolis, Portland, or Seattle. Hell, it lay situated in the shadows of two large cities, Chicago and Milwaukee. But now this tiny little hamlet on Lake Michigan was poised to host the latest flare-up in America's racial crack-up.

Almost immediately, the situation in the town of about 100,000 people began to degrade. According to livestreams, the protests had quickly turned to riots in two areas: near the scene of the Blake shooting and the downtown area of Kenosha. Windows were smashed at local businesses. Cars were set ablaze in a dealership parking lot. The Kenosha

County Courthouse was besieged by rioters. And a police officer was knocked out when some thug threw a brick at his head.

I sent an email to my bosses saying Kenosha was where I needed to be.

AUGUST 24

I landed in Milwaukee that afternoon with Jorge Ventura, a *Daily Caller* reporter I had gotten to know on the riot beat. By then reports had said the Wisconsin National Guard was going to be called out, but only about 200 soldiers were going to be activated. That was not nearly enough to support local law enforcement.

The Uber had trouble taking Jorge and me to downtown Kenosha. The main streets were blocked off with concrete barriers. Buildings in the downtown area that survived the previous night were boarded up. Despite people milling about and cars on the streets, Kenosha was eerily quiet. A lot of people were just driving by to see the destruction for themselves. It was hard for many to believe such damage was made in their sleepy little town overnight.

One of the boarded-up buildings included the office of the Kenosha County Democratic Party, complete with "Black Lives Matter" posters and "Vote Blue" banners.

Elijah Schaffer of *The Blaze*, another friend, gave us a quick recap of what he had seen and heard before we got there. According to Elijah, the city told business owners not to be downtown after 4:00 p.m. since they could not guarantee their safety.

He took us to the car dealership that had been set ablaze the first night. The air was thick with the smell of burnt metal and rubber. Amazingly, some cars somehow survived the inferno, although their windows were smashed and their doors dented. They would not survive the following night.

The sun was setting and a crowd that had gathered at Civic Center Park, across the street from the county courthouse, began a march, which took them all over town and residential areas. The crowd was peaceful, and I did not see them break anything or act in a violent way.

By the time they marched back downtown, it was dark. Shelby Talcott and Richie McGinniss, also with the *Daily Caller*, had stayed behind to monitor a different crowd gathering at the park. They told us around 8:20 p.m. rioters had started attacking the officers guarding the courthouse. We ran over, but not before I took a detour to grab my ballistic press vest. When I made it back to the courthouse, the officers had fired tear gas to push the rioters back. I had not yet received the gas mask I had ordered a few weeks earlier, so I really felt the effects of the irritant.

Some scattered, but the tear gas and other less-than-lethal ordnance failed to deter all the rioters. Many continued their battle with Kenosha police. Two armored police trucks drove up from behind the crowd, through the park, and moved into position in front of the courthouse to provide cover for the exposed line of officers.

At first it seemed the police had worn down the rioters. Things sort of died down. But then the crowd we had been following initially finally made its way back to the courthouse, providing reinforcements to the besieged shock troops. The crowd began throwing rocks and other objects at the police line, who returned fire with more crowd-control munitions.

People took cover across the street and behind the city garbage and dump trucks, which authorities had placed to prevent cars from driving through.

The problem with using city trucks as street barriers is that they became easy and inviting targets. Rioters broke vehicles' windows, doused the insides with accelerant, and tossed in matches or pieces of paper set on fire before running off. Nearly every truck the city had parked in the area was set ablaze that night.

Mirroring tactics from Antifa/black bloc groups in Portland, rioters used homemade shields and umbrellas to rush the police. Unlike the groups in Portland, the Kenosha rioters did not have the numbers or equipment to make full, mounted offensives.

Their small formations were easily repelled when police fired rubber bullets, flashbangs, and the like. One rioter in the formation was shot in the head with a less-than-lethal round. He dropped to the ground, screaming, while clutching his face. Street medics dragged him away to tend to him.

It was only 10:30 p.m., and the night's anarchy was far from over. Just then I finally saw a convoy of National Guardsmen making their way towards the courthouse. This would free up the police officers guarding the courthouse to be able to respond to the destruction now targeting buildings downtown, but it would still be another hour before law enforcement teams were dispatched.

Looking down the road, I saw fires in the car lot I had toured when I first arrived. Running down the street, I noticed the road and sidewalks were littered with glass from streetlights that had been torn down.

Arriving at the heavily hit car dealership, I saw rioters finishing the job from the night before. Every remaining car on the lot was on fire.

That wasn't the only blaze. Looking to the sky, I saw black smoke billowing from not too far away. The whole city seemed to be on fire.

The fires of Kenosha provided the most enduring visual of the 2020 riots—and perhaps the most damning indictment of the media. It was in Kenosha where CNN's Omar Jimenez gave a report to viewers that showed huge balls of fire engulfing buildings and cars behind him. Meanwhile the chyron rolling along the bottom of the screen told a different story: "FIERY BUT MOSTLY PEACEFUL PROTESTS AFTER POLICE SHOOTING."

There was nothing—and I mean *nothing*—even remotely peaceful about the protests that night or any other night in Kenosha.

I quickly ran several blocks, where I encountered more buildings on fire and looters "mostly peacefully" breaking into businesses. As I walked toward the closest business aflame, nearby three armed men in tactical gear were chasing rioters away. They confirmed my initial impression and said they were there to protect businesses from being damaged.

"We're trying to stop them from hurting their own community, man," one of the armed men told me.

"I understand why they're mad at the cops; they tried to murder one of their own people," another chimed in. "I understand it, but your neighbors didn't do shit to you."

The armed group's stated intentions to me were confirmed when rioters started damaging a different car dealership and repair shop. A tow truck was already on fire. People were jumping on the hoods of cars, smashing windshields and throwing rocks through the windows.

"Get off the fucking car!" a loud voice shouted. The crowd started scattering.

Then I saw one of the armed men I had just interviewed walking towards the lot, but without his rifle raised. That's all that was needed to stop rioters from attacking that particular business.

The problem is that I only saw three such heroes that night. They were far outnumbered by the hordes of rioters running around causing mayhem. A call to arms for like-minded reinforcements went out the next day, leading to the most explosive night of the riots, but more on that later.

At one business I saw, some rioters stayed outside to keep watch and prevent others from filming their friends ransacking the interior. They had used a large stone to smash in the glass door.

There were so many fires the air was saturated with smoke. The Community Corrections Division, the town's probation office, was also broken into and set on fire. I reached that building as the office's American flag was waving in front of the flames.

The rope on the flagpole burned, dropping the flag to the ground. I tried to go over to pick it up but was stopped by police setting up a perimeter so fire crews could safely respond to the burning buildings.

Thankfully, a man who was livestreaming and who was on the other side of the perimeter being established was able to pick it up. He had no idea who I was. Amazingly, he trusted me enough to hold the phone with which he was livestreaming so he could safely put the flag in his bag.

I made sure those watching knew the flag, America's symbol that many hold dear, would be ok in the midst of the unrest.

Moments later, I encountered a man who had come out of his house to witness the night's anarchy.

"You thinking about getting a gun?" I asked him.

"Thinking about it," he chuckled, adding he believed the people destroying the town were not from Kenosha.

When I got back to the intersection where the first torched car dealership had stood, vehicles in a nearby municipal parking lot were on fire. It was starting to spread in a daisy chain. This was gravely concerning because this lot was right next to a home.

"Get out of the house!" some people in a crowd were shouting. The lights were off, and it appeared no one was inside. Thankfully, the car fires burned out before reaching the vehicles parked right next to the home.

It was now past midnight. Firefighters, with heavy police escort, were finally coming out in force to respond to the blazes. Because there were so many infernos, they had to prioritize, which meant often driving by the smaller ones. The smoke-filled main road looked like a scene out of the "Walking Dead" or "I Am Legend," with trash and broken glass all over the ground and buildings covered in graffiti.

Back at the courthouse, I saw the National Guard had positioned their Humvees alongside the sheriff's department's armored trucks to bolster their defenses. The ground was littered with the rocks, bricks, bottles, and other objects that had been thrown at them.

"Fucking Pigs" was scrawled in graffiti on the sidewalk directly in front of the police line.

A few people were still hanging around, mainly heckling the officers and soldiers, but did not physically attack them. It was very late (or very early, depending on your view) and finally much quieter, save for the occasional siren from police and fire vehicles. After taking video of another garbage truck on fire, I called it a night around 2:30 a.m.

AUGUST 25

By the time I got back out into the streets the next morning, city crews were hard at work cleaning up the mess. Some of the broken glass had been swept and a few of the torn-down streetlights had been taken away. Not much was happening at the courthouse, so I checked out some of the businesses that had been targeted by the rioters. Storeowners and community members were also busy cleaning up.

I approached the charred remains of a recently thriving business. I found the owner, Scott Carpenter, and waited to conduct an interview with him. As Scott was speaking to a local news outlet, his mother, Linda, walked up to him in tears.

"It's all gone," she said, sobbing. "We didn't do anything to nobody. It's still burning."

Scott told me his father had started their store, B&L Office Furniture Inc., some 40 years ago in their garage. They had called that particular brick and mortar location home for more than 30 of those 40 years. The B and L represented his parents' first names.

"We service the city and the city's been really good to us, so I know it wasn't somebody from around here," Linda said. "It has to be someplace else."

Scott was at a loss for explanation, or for what B&L's future held. "I don't know what's next. What do we do next, other than clean up, and I have some loose ends with some customers that we have going on, but otherwise, you know, I hate to say it, I'm still thinking, my Dad [would say] 'We still have some business that we got to take care of.' We just can't leave our other customers hanging that have things waiting on us. But I feel saddened because this is done." He gestured to the burned-out building. "It's done."

"We're gonna try to keep working. We're gonna try to either get another small place temporarily, and we want our customers to know we're still here for them," Linda said.

"We still have a job to do, but as far as this building—it's a complete loss," Scott said.

I asked Scott what his response is to people who always try to downplay damage done to private property because there is insurance. It's a common argument by leftists that property damage is no big deal, especially compared to violence that maims or kills people (particularly killings by police officers).

"It's not justifiable," he said. "We have insurance, yeah, but the insurance isn't there so somebody can destroy your things…. We pay for insurance. It causes insurance rates to go up. It's basically theft. Whoever did this stole from us, and that raises the cost of everything."

Linda chimed in. "I don't think it's justified for anyone to ruin anybody else's property. It's against the law; they ought to be put in prison or [be] made to pay back what they've destroyed."

"Doing this isn't going to help your cause," said Scott. "In my opinion, doing this [points to the rubble] silences your cause; you are not making the cause look good. You're going to get further with honey than you are with vinegar, proven fact." Scott warned that the business owners who had weathered the storm so far needed to be ready. More destruction was almost certain to happen.

A woman whose office down the street had been damaged was similarly upset. "It's sickening, this is sickening. This is disgraceful, and this is not going to solve any problems. Black lives matter? All lives matter, people. Let's get it together. Let's work together. We are in hard times; you guys are making it harder than it has to be. My God! [Linda] has been working at a furniture store for 50 years [and now] has nothing and because why? Because a police officer made a bad choice! Don't take it out on the innocent people! All we want to do is come to work and help people out."

She bitterly criticized the drivers slowing down to take pictures and video of the damage for laughs. "When there's no unemployment and you can't get food stamps, don't come crying to us, you goddamn losers."[30]

Later that afternoon, Jacob Blake's family held a press conference with their lawyers to provide an update on his condition. What stuck out to me most was how Blake was able to even survive after getting shot seven times at close range. According to one of his attorneys, Blake was partially paralyzed, had holes in his stomach, suffered damage to his kidneys and liver, and had his entire colon and much of his small intestines removed, in addition to being shot in the arm.

Just like the other days, all we had to do was wait until night for the riots to kick off. During the day, a fence was erected at the courthouse. It appeared to be the exact type used to defend the federal courthouse in Portland.

I got to the county courthouse around 8:20 p.m. to find a crowd of protesters marching close to the fence.

One young woman holding a small American flag shouted, "Kill the fucking police! Kill them back!" She then asked someone for a lighter. One man obliged her request, but because of the flag's material, it would melt instead of burn. The man pulled out a bottle of whiskey and drenched the flag. They were finally able to set it on fire to great cheers.

"Death to Americaaaa!" the woman screamed as the man threw the burning stick over the fence.

For good measure, the woman repeatedly kicked the fence. This performance energized the crowd. They began violently shaking the fence, attempting to tear it down in the same manner as the rioters in Portland.

The only police officers in evidence were perched on the roof. But as protesters threatened to knock over the fence protecting the courthouse, officers swarmed from inside the building to do battle. Just like that, the night's chaos was on.

It looked like the night would unfold much like all the others. Rioters would attack officers, hurling an array of rocks and fireworks and other projectiles at them. The police would respond with warnings that would be disregarded, then action designed to repel and disperse the rioters. Tear gas. Rubber bullets. Flashbangs. Pepper balls. Other first responders would frantically try to contain the fires and other destruction meant for no other reason than to destroy. Rioters would clash with police through the night while smashing and breaking whatever suited them, and possibly stealing whatever they found attractive to take. As the long night wore on, the wild destructive crowds would melt away. By the time the morning sun was approaching, "order" would have been restored.

Rinse. Reset. Repeat. Night after night.

There was a sameness to it that I had seen throughout my tour of America's ravaged urban centers. I wouldn't say I had grown bored of it— far from it. But I had been lulled into a sense that each night was like the one before, with the same tragic opera playing out, no matter the stage.

I was wrong. This night would turn out to be unlike any of the others. It would cement Kenosha, Wisconsin, firmly in the nation's consciousness for decades to come. And it would further sharpen America's divide about the kind of country we live in, and how we're all supposed to get along.

It started out as another night of violence and mayhem, much like the rest. But there was one key difference: Given the city's inability to prevent the destruction and vandalism of the previous few evenings, some civic-minded citizens thought it best to arm up to protect peoples' livelihoods from further damage throughout the evening.

After the typical skirmishes between rioters and police, law enforcement once more set about dispersing the crowds at the courthouse.

One thinning group of rioters was driven south down Sheridan Road. Around the intersection of Sheridan Road and 60th Street, they encountered a group of armed civilians guarding an Ultimate gas station.

When I arrived, the armed group and the crowd were engaged in a tense verbal confrontation. I do not know who started it, but seeing as how most, if not all, of the civilians were white and armed with rifles and shotguns, it most likely did not sit well with the crowd of rioters.

I heard the armed civilians tell the crowd they supported their right to protest, but they were not going to let them burn down or break into any more stores.

As I filmed the arguments between the two groups, one of the rioters brandished a handgun. Meanwhile, a short, white man in a red shirt, later identified as Joseph Rosenbaum, taunted the armed civilians, yelling, "Shoot me, nigga! Shoot me, nigga…Bust on me, nigga, for real!"

Someone on the rioting side then set a dumpster on fire and attempted to roll it down the street towards the armored police vehicles just on the other side of the intersection. A man from the armed civilian side put it out with a fire extinguisher. This further angered the rioters, leading to more heated arguments.

In a move that I can only describe as them wanting to de-escalate the situation, the armed civilians moved across the street to a Gulf gas station as a police convoy patrolled nearby.

The crowd followed and harassed the police convoy until the armored trucks pushed them back south on Sheridan Road once again. Since the police were coming back into the area, the armed civilians did not see themselves as needed at that location. They moved away from the Gulf station. It was the last time I saw the group that night.

I ran off to film a video of a pile of tires that were on fire at the car dealership on 60th Street. When I walked back to the Sheridan Road intersection, the rioters and police were engaged in a tense, though typical, standoff.

For a short period of time—five, maybe ten minutes?—nothing dramatic happened. The crowd faced the police. The police stared back. I honestly thought things likely were done for the night since the crowd had decreased in size, and the police were no longer advancing south.

Then we all heard gunshots ring out, originating south of the intersection. Acting as the rational person I am, I started to run down the street, *toward* the gunshots.

As I approached 61st Street, I saw a young man in a green shirt with a rifle running in the opposite direction. The young man was Kyle Rittenhouse. People were chasing after him, shouting that he had just shot someone.

While I grabbed my phone to start recording the chase, a man in a hoodie, Anthony Huber, swiped at Rittenhouse with a skateboard. I can't say for sure if the skateboard made hard contact with Rittenhouse, but the skateboard flew from Huber's hands, landing on the left side of the street. My phone started to record the interaction as Huber rushed over to pick up his skateboard, where, at the same time, Rittenhouse fell to the ground.

"Get his ass!" someone shouted.

Someone ran up to Rittenhouse to jump kick him. I could see and hear Rittenhouse fire two shots. Huber came up right after the attempted kick and hit Rittenhouse with his skateboard. Huber's momentum carried him past Rittenhouse, but not before I could see Huber reach behind to grab the rifle.

Rittenhouse fired another shot. I saw Huber drop his skateboard, reach for his chest, and fall to the ground.

At this point I couldn't know what Rittenhouse was going to do or if more people were going to rush or shoot him in an attempt to stop him. I backed away down 61st Street, hearing more gunshots from what I believed to be in front of me and definitely close behind me. People were scattering in all directions.

"They're in their car!" a woman shouted. More gunshots rang out while a car raced past.

"Oh fuck, are people doing drive-bys?"

I tried to find hard cover to get behind, but there was almost nothing except for a parked car. I knelt down by the engine block. I stayed there for about a minute before a man came out of a house across the street and yelled at me to get away from his car.

"Sorry, I'm just trying to find some cover," I told him, still trying to grasp the magnitude of a situation with multiple shootings in which I now found myself.

"Go find cover somewhere else!" he shouted back.

The police, who had been up the street the entire time, started to come down the road in my direction. On my phone I was trying to find the *Daily Caller* crew. Shelby told me she was by the hospital, and Richie was at the scene of the first shooting. I avoided Sheridan Road, moving carefully south on 10th Ave. About halfway down 10th Ave, more gunshots rang out.

"What the hell is going on?"

By the time I got to 63rd Street, police were pouring in and setting up a perimeter at the car dealership parking lot where the first gunshots were fired.

"Hey, I saw some of the shooting!" I told the officers, thinking it could get me through to the other side of the perimeter so I could get to Shelby.

"You saw the shooting?" an officer asked.

"Yes, sir."

He told me to come to him, and he found a Kenosha police officer so I could give a statement. I then showed them the video I took of the shooting that I had already posted to my Twitter account.

After giving them my business card, I was allowed to leave, but not out the way I had hoped. I had to cut across 62nd Street back to Sheridan Road to head south. I found Shelby on the corner across the street from the parking lot. A car in the lot was on fire.

That's when I found out Richie had not just been at the scene of the shooting, but damn near got shot himself. Richie had been so close to the action he ended up taking Rosenbaum to the hospital. That's where police were interviewing him.

We went to the hospital to try to find out how much longer Richie would be talking to the police. We waited outside the main doors and sat down for the first time in hours. That's when the adrenaline that had been pumping in my system started to wear off, and the craziness of what I just saw started to really hit me.

"Did I almost get shot? I think I almost got shot?"

"Watched someone die, that's a new one."

"Guess I got to call Mom to let her know I'm okay."

While we waited outside the hospital, a man on the verge of tears was nearby talking on his phone. From what Shelby and I could gather, it appeared as though the man knew the third person shot by Rittenhouse, Gaige Grosskreutz. He was in distress at the thought of his friend possibly losing his arm.

The man ranted how it was probably a white supremacist who committed the shootings. Shelby and I looked at each other in confusion since there was no evidence at that moment to support such a claim. My hope to interview the man was crushed after he hung up the phone and shouted, to no one in particular, "No one fucking talk to me!"

When we found it was going to be hours before Richie was going to be done talking with the cops, we decided to head back to our hotel. It was now around 2:00 in the morning. While walking back, we saw a convoy of vehicles moving down the road. I noticed many of the cars had flat tires.

"Wow, those are some flat tires," I semi-joked.

"Yeah, the police slashed our tires," said someone with their windows down.

"Where are you guys heading to?" I asked.

"We're all from Milwaukee."

"Well, how are you getting back to Milwaukee?" I then asked.

"We're just trying to get out of Kenosha."

"Yeah," I said. "That's probably a good idea."

I had been talking with various BBC news programs throughout my time in Kenosha, and they were just waking up to news of the shootings. I got back to my hotel room to do my first appearance on British T.V. to retell what I had just seen.

AUGUST 26

I got around four hours of sleep. When I woke up, my phone was filled with messages that had been sent by different news organizations, some from around the world, all asking about the shootings, which was now the lead story.

I started to comb through the videos that had been posted to gather what exactly happened. People were replying to my tweet that showed the verbal confrontations before the shootings, saying I had captured all three who were shot in a 1 minute and 30 second video.

The mood in Kenosha changed drastically the following evening for the night's protests, and that's what it was, a protest. I did not see any major acts of violence, nor did I see officers have to come out of the county courthouse. The only thing protesters seemed be violating was curfew. The crowd was significantly smaller than in previous nights. The group continued to march in the street and started to head west, but there was some debate on where to head next.

One black man got the crowd to start heading to the east because that's where all the white people and police officers live. The protesters stopped near the intersection where Huber and Grosskreutz were shot. Huber's girlfriend, Hannah Gittings, was crying. Through tears, she gave a speech to the protesters.

"I just want to say, that Anthony Huber was one of the most amazing people that ever walked this fucking Earth. He had nothing but love in his heart for this city, and that's why we were fucking out here last night. And he took down an armed gunman with nothing but his fucking skateboard, and he took that fucking bullet." She broke down in tears again, cutting her address short.

After chanting, "What was his name? Anthony Huber!" repeatedly, the protesters held a moment of silence.

The crowd and a small car caravan marched through the eastern neighborhoods of Kenosha, near the lakefront. It was late. They called for people to come out of their homes to join the protest. When the crowd marched back downtown, one young man broke off and started to spray paint "Free Palestine" and "BLM" in the driveway of the Beth Hillel Temple, one of the only synagogues in Kenosha.

Someone else then tagged "BLM" onto a sign for Christ the King Church. The video of the synagogue being vandalized drew sharp criticisms from the Jewish community, though there were some others who said it was the synagogue's fault since it had the Israeli flag flying underneath the American flag.

Beth Hillel Temple is a fairly progressive synagogue. Rabbi Dena Feingold did not muster much outrage for the relatively minor vandalism.

"We are advocates for justice for all oppressed people," the rabbi told Jewish News Syndicate. "We support the movement for black lives, and we know that one person with a can of spray paint does not speak for an entire cause. We pray for Jacob Blake and decry the vigilante murders that took place a block from our synagogue two nights ago. Our call is for justice and peace in our community and around the world."[31]

My time in Kenosha, as short as it was, certainly changed me in many ways. The physical signs of little sleep, constant stress, and lots of physical activity were obvious.

When I appeared on *Tucker Carlson Tonight* after I flew back to Washington, D.C. on August 27th, the bags under my eyes had grown in size.

"It looks scary as hell from the pictures," Tucker said. "Was it?" I responded that, at the time, Kenosha would only be behind Minneapolis in terms of the absolute chaos I'd experienced during my reporting.

Minneapolis was still number one in my book because the riots there were on a much larger scale. In all truth, I was scared during the now-famous moment in Kenosha.

The Rittenhouse incident was certainly now the main takeaway from the Kenosha riots, thus making it more important than ever to understand what happened the night of August 25th.

As with anything controversial, people immediately pounced, seized, and jumped to conclusions.

In the first few hours after the shootings, I made a point to not say anything about them publicly beyond what I saw, whether with my own eyes or videos that I, and others, had taken.

By the afternoon of the following day, I still had no exact idea what led to Rittenhouse shooting Rosenbaum, which then resulted in him shooting Huber and Grosskreutz. It seemed to me an argument could easily be made that Rittenhouse shot in self-defense. Still, there were those making the case the crowd was justified for attacking Rittenhouse because he had just killed someone, and they did not know if he would continue to kill random people. It all hinged on if Rittenhouse shot in self-defense at the very beginning.

Before any facts were known, accusations made by Democrats and people in the mainstream media charged Rittenhouse with being a domestic terrorist, a white supremacist even, who crossed state lines with a rifle with the intent to kill peaceful protesters. As shown from the man on the phone outside the hospital barely two hours after the shootings, the "white supremacist" claim spread far and wide.

"A 17-year-old white supremacist domestic terrorist drove across state lines, armed with an AR 15," Rep. Ayanna Pressley (D-MA) tweeted. "He shot and killed 2 people who had assembled to affirm the value, dignity, and worth of Black lives. Fix your damn headlines."

When Pressley posted that tweet, there was no solid evidence Rittenhouse had driven across state lines with an AR-15 or that he was a white supremacist. Some pointed to how he had posted "Blue Lives Matter" pictures on his social media as proof, but that is not enough to support such a serious charge in any sane realm. There is still no proof to back up such incendiary claims. In fact, the only person we can say for sure who used racial slurs was Rosenbaum. ("Shoot me, nigga!")

The white supremacist claim was so widespread, an internal Department of Homeland Security memo written right after the shootings to brief top officials on the situation noted, "Media are trying to craft the narrative of a police-obsessed lone wolf. Democrats labeled him a white supremacist with zero evidence."

The biggest problem with the white supremacist claim is the color of three people who Rittenhouse shot: All white men. There were plenty of opportunities for the entire group of armed civilians, not just Rittenhouse, to start mowing down the crowd of rioters—keyword being rioters—and yet they did not do so. As stated before, it even appeared they removed themselves from the angry crowd to lessen the possibility of a violent confrontation.

Rosenbaum, Huber, and Grosskreutz were in Kenosha for different reasons.

Rosenbaum had the worst past of the three that we know. *The Washington Post* reported he had been molested by his alcoholic stepfather on an "almost daily basis." He was sent to a group home after his mother was sent to jail, where he started to use heroin and methamphetamine. At the age of 18, he was sent to prison for most of the next 14 years because he sexually assaulted at least five preteen boys.

After being released from prison in Arizona, Rosenbaum met and fathered a child with a woman who moved to Kenosha. He moved to the town to be with her. He spent the next couple of years being homeless with another woman he met in a hospital.

Rosenbaum attacked his girlfriend in a domestic dispute and subsequently tried to overdose on pills. Kenosha police found him convulsing, and he was sent to the hospital for treatment. After a few days, he was released on the night of August 25. While he went to visit his now-fiancé, she told him he could not stay the night because of the no-contact order. She warned him to not go downtown, but he somehow made his way to the gas station.

The *Post* also reported on Huber's troubled past. A native of Kenosha, his girlfriend claims they were at the riot to record what was happening in the downtown area since Huber had been friends with Blake. Huber's mother was a hoarder—a constant stress in his life—and he suffered from bipolar disorder.

According to the *Post*: "In 2012, Huber brandished a butcher knife and threatened to 'gut' his brother 'like a pig' if he didn't clean the house. The family told police that Huber choked his brother with his hands for 10 seconds before letting him go and retreating to the skate park. Convicted of strangulation and false imprisonment, he was placed on probation but violated the terms and was sent to prison in 2017. When he came home, he got into another argument over the state of the house. This time, he kicked his sister, and went back to prison on a charge of disorderly conduct in 2018."

Huber eventually gained ownership of the house after his mother was evicted, and his uncle, the owner, charged him with cleaning up the place. In the aftermath of the Blake shooting, Huber had already attended the protests and riots that occurred on August 25.

Grosskreutz attended many of the protests in Milwaukee as a street medic by the time of the Blake shooting. When things started to pop off in nearby Kenosha, about 40 miles south of Milwaukee, Grosskreutz headed there. That is why he was on the streets that night and even filmed Rittenhouse as he ran away, but more on that later.[32]

When I watched the armed group of civilians vacate the Gulf station on Sheridan Road because the police were approaching, I did not see Rittenhouse among them, and that was the last time I saw the group. Rittenhouse was separate from the group because, according to him, he was not with them to begin with.

Then there was a five-to-ten minute gap from the time the armed group left the Gulf gas station to the first set of gunshots.

In videos from bystanders and reporter Drew Hernandez, Rittenhouse is seen being chased by Rosenbaum into the parking lot of the car dealership. Rosenbaum threw the plastic bag containing socks, underwear, and deodorant the hospital had given him when he was discharged. Two videos taken at different angles showed *someone else* shot a gun before Rittenhouse fired the rifle he was carrying.

That someone was Joshua Ziminski. Ziminski was the man I had filmed earlier in the night brandishing a handgun while the rioters and armed civilians argued at the first gas station. In October, several months after the events of August 25, 2020, Ziminski was charged with disorderly conduct-use of a dangerous weapon for firing what he claimed was a warning shot. (Ziminski pleaded not guilty; as of publication his trial had not begun.) He also claimed the handgun from that night has since been stolen.[33]

Ziminski firing his gun appears to be one of the factors that explains Rittenhouse going from flight mode into fight mode. At that point, his avenues of escape were cut off due to the cars lined up in the parking lot.

My friend Richie was near Rittenhouse and Rosenbaum in the parking lot. He said because Rittenhouse was armed, he was drawing a lot of negative attention.

After the first gun shot, he said, Rittenhouse "went from running away to aiming his weapon," with Rosenbaum lunging to grab the rifle.

Then Rittenhouse fired four times, with Richie stepping just out of the line of fire. This is where the narrative of Rittenhouse being there to just indiscriminately kill people starts to fall apart. Instead of continuing shooting after Rosenbaum falls down, Rittenhouse looks over what had just happened, makes a phone call, and starts running towards the police stationed up Sheridan Road.

Grosskreutz was livestreaming and running behind Rittenhouse. He asked him, "You shot somebody?"

"I'm going to the police," Rittenhouse replied.

People can be heard in the background of Grosskreutz's video saying the guy he was chasing had just shot Rosenbaum.

"Hey, stop him!" Grosskreutz shouted as he continued to run after Rittenhouse.[34]

This is where I saw Rittenhouse and much of the action that unfolded. I started moving backwards onto 61st Street, where a fence partially blocked my view. So I did not see Rittenhouse shoot Grosskreutz in the arm after he shot Huber.

Luckily, journalist Brendan Gutenschwager, also known by his Twitter name @BGOnTheScene, continued to move up Sheridan Road to capture where I had left off.[35]

In the video Brendan captured, Rittenhouse, prior to falling down, was hit in the back of the head by someone who ran up to him. Rittenhouse's white hat fell off after the blow, but Rittenhouse did not shoot him.

After the shooting of Huber, Brendan's video showed Grosskreutz approaching Rittenhouse with his hands up. You can see Rittenhouse determining to not shoot Grosskreutz at first because it looked as though he was not a threat. Grosskreutz then darts off to the side and starts to aim the handgun in his right hand at Rittenhouse. Rittenhouse fired off one round, which destroyed Grosskreutz's upper right bicep.

Another person who was close behind Grosskreutz held his hands up and started to back away. Grosskreutz was still livestreaming when he got shot after he pointed his handgun at Rittenhouse's head. Once again, instead of continuing shooting random people around him, Rittenhouse looked around to see if anyone else was going to attack him, got up, and tried to surrender to the approaching police convoy.

I found out Grosskreutz was shot after another freelance photographer who stayed at the scene texted me the video he took of Grosskreutz's wounds. A portion of Grosskreutz's bicep was just gone. It took about another minute before police arrived to give first aid and transport Grosskreutz to the hospital.

This is where I have to issue a slight correction to what I originally told the Associated Press the next morning: "A witness, Julio Rosas, 24, said that when the gunman stumbled, 'two people jumped onto him and there was a struggle for control of his rifle. At that point during the struggle, he just began to fire multiple rounds, and that dispersed people near him...The rifle was being jerked around in all directions while it was being fired.'"[36]

As I previously stated, I thought Rittenhouse was still shooting after I kneeled behind the parked car's engine block, but that was disproven by Brendan's video; Rittenhouse only fired one more time after shooting Huber.

Rewatching the video I took, I realized I had mistakenly believed some of the gunshots that were being fired behind me to be occurring in the street in front of me due to the echo from the houses.

––––––––––––––––––––

Whether it was unwise for Rittenhouse to be in Kenosha, with him repeatedly stating his intentions to protect people's livelihoods from further destruction, does not matter. He was there. Arguing over that fact is a coulda, woulda, shoulda.

Whether Rittenhouse should or should not have been in town also does not negate the facts of the night, backed up by multiple videos from different people, showing that he only shot those who attacked him first. He even took pains to *not* shoot at least one person who punched him in the head while he ran away. He had an interaction with Grosskreutz and did not shoot him initially because at first, Grosskreutz was not trying to shoot him.

According to a Facebook post from Jacob Marshall, a friend of Grosskreutz who visited him in the hospital, Grosskreutz said his only regret from that night "was not killing the kid and hesitating to pull the gun before emptying the entire mag into him. Coward." Marshall later deleted the comment after it gained significant attention on social media.

In an analysis from the *Washington Post*, they noted how Rosenbaum was helping push the on-fire dumpster towards the police convoy before the fire was put out by the armed civilians. I filmed Huber being confrontational towards the armed civilians, right behind Rosenbaum at the first gas station.

The *Post* reported that some of the armed civilians had pointed their guns at the rioting crowd when the rioters were first pushed back by police, but I did not see that happening when I approached the situation (which, admittedly, was already underway). I did not see any from the armed civilian side point their rifles directly at someone, though given how much was happening, it is possible that it did occur but I missed it.

The narrative that Rittenhouse traveled across a state line with the rifle he used during the shootings to go to a town where he had no connections has been proven to be false, as well.

Rittenhouse gave his $1,200 COVID-19 relief check to his friend Dominick Black, who lived in Wisconsin, to purchase the rifle for him (Black was over 18). The rifle stayed in Black's stepdad's house until the riots happened. It was Black who asked Rittenhouse to help guard the businesses downtown. Rittenhouse, who had worked as a lifeguard in Kenosha, knew the city well.[37]

"Our job is to protect this business, and part of my job is to also help people," Rittenhouse told the *Daily Caller* in a video interview recorded before the shooting. "There's somebody hurt, I'm running into harm's way; that's why I have my rifle because I have to protect myself, obviously. I also have my medkit."[38]

In other interviews he conducted before the shootings, Rittenhouse repeatedly stated his desire to help anyone who was injured. That hardly sounds like someone who was looking for any justification to shoot people.

The idea that Rittenhouse, along with all the other members of the armed group, went to Kenosha to shoot random protesters is not backed up, based on what other reporters and I saw and recorded that night. And the narrative holding that Rosenbaum and Huber were simply peaceful protesters who were shot for no reason is also debunked from videos taken that night.

I'm not blind to the fact that I do have a bias towards gun rights. I approve of people lawfully protecting their livelihoods from rioting mobs when police abandon their posts or are overwhelmed. We all have our opinions. That said, I am capable of putting my biases aside to report the facts on the ground.

If I had seen Rittenhouse acting as the aggressor, going out of his way to attack innocent people over the course of the night, I would have reported that. But numerous videos posted from multiple people fail to support such claims. I encourage everyone to look through videos from that night before forming an opinion.

Much of the fault for creating the situation that ended up with Kyle Rittenhouse shooting three people and killing two lies with state and government officials in Wisconsin. That includes local police.

Law enforcement did not have the numbers or the will to fully enforce the curfew and maintain order. Or perhaps the local police were ordered to not arrest people who were rioting—it's still not clear at this point.

What *is* clear is that with the abject failure of authorities to maintain order and ensure public safety—creating a power vacuum that existed for days—some private citizens felt compelled to step up themselves and protect what parts of Kenosha they could.

This is not to say the shootings were completely avoidable, but law enforcement not having the numbers, the will, or the orders to forcefully end the riots before they got out of hand for continuous days all but guaranteed something insane would happen. And it did.

Kyle Rittenhouse has been accused of being a vigilante. A vigilante, as we all know, is someone who takes the law into his own hands. Someone who doesn't let the system dispense justice as designed, who preempts the duties of government officials.

But what happens when those entrusted to enforce the laws and to protect the populace refuse to do so? Does taking steps to protect oneself and one's community make one a hero? Or a villain? The nation will be debating that question for a long time.

One of the more interesting stories of the Kenosha riots centers on the presence of those armed civilians who showed up to protect businesses. There is no question they prevented even more destruction by their vigilant presence.

I was able to interview one such member after he reached out to me. We'll call him Boone.

Boone, who lives in Wisconsin, said he went to Kenosha because he knew the anarchy was going to continue. He wanted to do his part to prevent his part of the country from descending into further chaos.

"I felt compelled to do something, you know?" he said. "I knew the police were in over their head, and it was proven right when we got down there." Boone recalled how the police interacted with them earlier in the night. They did not say they appreciated what Boone and his compatriots were doing. But they also did not tell the group go away.

Boone was in town on the 24th, but not on the 25th. He thought that, given how out of control the situation was when he was there, the authorities surely would bring in the reinforcements necessary to restore order. Had they done so, it is almost certain people would not have died.

Like many of those who made up the armed citizens brigades in Kenosha, Boone said he absolutely supports people's right to peacefully protest, but he draws the line at rioting and looting.

"My first reaction was to leave the team over at the gas station. I immediately started yelling at people to get away from the gas station. We knew there were people there who were going to be using gas to be arsonists. When I walked up, there were already three people trying to break open the ATM. So I immediately scattered the crowd."

Boone said they also wanted to hold down the two gas stations on Sheridan Road to prevent anyone from setting fire to them, which would have caused enormous damage had they exploded.

"We only left that spot because two police cruisers came up the street, and they scattered some of the remnants that were behind the march. We knew we could leave, and the police would have control of that location."

While I was still up near the courthouse, Jorge filmed the moment of the armed men protecting the gas station and an agitator, a black woman, screaming at them.

"I'm all for protests, but you can't be destroying your neighbors' houses and businesses," an armed man wearing cowboy boots said.

"Bitch, you're not for protesting and you don't give a fuck," the woman screamed back, adding, "Fuck you, you're not with us!"

Boone said he heard some gunfire close by when his group was near B&L Office Furniture Inc. and the two car lots. Citing his U.S. Army combat experience that included tours in the Middle East, he said he knows what gunfire sounds like.

It was at this point during the night's events that I arrived and saw someone disperse the rioters trying to destroy the cars at Real C & M Automotive & Truck Repair. It was Boone.

"So just to make it clear, you're not a white supremacist, and you weren't there to intimidate the peaceful protesters?" I asked him.

"No, I think [that assertion] is ridiculous," Boone replied. "We had no intention of interacting aggressively with the police or aggressively against the protesters. The rioters, on the other hand, we would if we had to, react aggressively, because they were committing violence against the city of Kenosha."

He added he hadn't had to shoot his rifle that night, but emphasized Americans have the right to self-defense.

"When dangerous groups decide to come to your city to burn it down or to destroy it or to do whatever, commit violence against your town, you should not be surprised that there are people there who are going to want to protect where they work or where they live. And if you are [a] criminal, which these people were, and armed citizens who are defending their town, you know, take action against you, don't be surprised if it's violence that ends the threat that they are posing to your town."

He did have an issue, however, with why Kyle Rittenhouse was alone. "Even I wouldn't go into that situation alone. You're just asking to be overwhelmed by an angry mob that is not looking for reasonable conversation."

I arrived bright and early at the Kenosha County Courthouse for jury selection in the Kyle Rittenhouse trial on November 1, 2021. While it was not my first time in Kenosha since the riots, being back this time was an odd feeling. I felt a mixture of nostalgia and shock at how peaceful things were in the same areas where mayhem and anarchy had reigned the previous summer. Yet Kenosha still bore the scars of the riots.

I covered the trial every day for Townhall. I won't bore you with every detail of the trial since it never should have gone to trial in the first place and I've already explained what happened. The jury saw it the same way I did: Rittenhouse was innocent because it was self-defense.

While I knew the most important aspects of the case, the trial helped fill in several gaps from that hectic night:

- The reason Rittenhouse ended up by himself is that Ryan Balch, an Army veteran who was assigned to watch his back, lost track of him at the Ultimate gas station.

- After being separated from Balch, Rittenhouse got a call from Black, who said there was a fire at the car lot at 63rd Street and Sheridan Road. Rittenhouse was sent to put it out. Rittenhouse said he asked a random person to go with him but all they did was give him a fire extinguisher.
- Rittenhouse did not cross state lines with the AR-15 nor was he dropped off by his mom.
- Kenosha local Lucas Zanin and his stepdaughter were parked across from the Car Source lot, confirming the lot was being attacked by the time Rittenhouse approached, when he was then ambushed by Rosenbaum.
- Kenosha police detectives drove around to ensure the gas station pumps were turned off to prevent rioters and arsonists from having easy access to gasoline. This was not known to the general public at the time of the riots. Detectives also testified they noticed cars were coming into town without license plates.
- Rittenhouse and other defense witnesses, including a former employee of Car Source, testified they were asked by Sahil and Anmol Khindri, whose family owns the business, to protect the remaining buildings and inventory. The Khindris denied asking for help.
- Sahil did say he was not scared of the armed men when they showed up on the night of August 25th. In fact, Sahil said he thought it was so cool seeing the firearms and gear he wanted to get a picture of the group, which included Rittenhouse and Black.
- Grosskreutz's concealed carry permit was expired on August 25th, 2020. While I was covering the chaos in Kenosha, my friends had taken a week-long excursion to the shore in New Jersey. I arrived home first from Milwaukee before my roommates, Logan Hall and Greg Price.

MILWAUKEE AFTERMATH

Being in Kenosha for the riots made the Rittenhouse trial an eye opening experience in many ways. Watching Assistant District Attorney Thomas Binger attempt to put an innocent man in prison for the rest of his life certainly helped me understand why people hate lawyers so much. It seemed to me that Binger had no case, so he tried to throw anything at the wall hoping something would stick. He tried to enter into evidence Rittenhouse saying on video he wanted to shoot suspected looters with his AR-15 weeks before the riots. Rightfully, Judge Bruce Schroeder said those were two different incidents and ruled that Binger was not allowed to bring it up. Binger tried mentioning it in front of the jury anyway, because, in my opinion, he was both desperate and a bad prosecutor.

This was obvious when Richie testified. Binger tried to discredit Richie by saying he had no idea what Rosenbaum was going to do to Rittenhouse before being shot, calling it "complete guesswork."

"Well [Rosenbaum] screamed, 'Fuck you' and reached for the weapon," Richie replied in a deadpan manner. It was certainly a satisfying moment.

I met with Richie for dinner after he testified to catch up and to congratulate him on finally being able to close this chapter of his life.

It was the first time Richie had been back in Kenosha since the riots. Before he testified, he toured the town, including the Car Source lots.

"I ended up where the shooting happened...I still very much felt like it was unfinished business. My role in this situation wasn't over yet," he said.

When he was finished with his testimony, Richie left the courthouse, got into the car he was using and called his Mom.

"When I realized it was all done, I just kind of lost it," he explained. "I've been trying to remain stoic for the purpose of serving my role and not ruining my public image and all these things that are at play...My Mom said, 'Your Dad would be so proud of you.'"

While it is easy for people (including me) who were not behind Rosenbaum when he was shot to say good riddance to a pedophile being killed, it's understandable Richie does not necessarily see it that way. At the time, he didn't know Rosenbaum's history. All he saw was a man dying in the street.

"Everybody can say what they think but when [Rosenbaum] looked at me, I could see the panic in his eyes. I felt the panic in his soul as I was cradling him. So people can say he had a death wish or this or that but there's one thing I can take from this, it doesn't matter what someone's politics are, it doesn't matter if someone is good or bad, every human being is born in the image of God. And same thing with Rittenhouse, there's a loss of innocence that happens to everybody as they grow old...When I said, 'We're gonna have a beer after this, man. Everything is going to be okay. We're gonna have a beer after this and we're gonna laugh about this.' I'm looking at him in the eyes trying to keep him comfortable, I wouldn't take that back because that moment to me was probably his last cognizant moment."

What angered and disturbed me the most after the verdict was how, even after the trial was publicly available, many people in the country still believed in the false narratives that were peddled for more than a year. The media still couldn't get the environment in which the shootings took place right. They kept calling it a "protest" instead of what it actually was, a riot. I was most shocked to hear how some were finding out for the first time that Rittenhouse did not kill black people, even though that was one of the easiest things to prove right after the shootings. It highlighted for me just how powerful the mainstream media and social media can be when they are unchallenged.

I felt the gaslighting myself shortly after the shootings. While what I witnessed was clearly self-defense, the coverage and conversation around that night was so biased against Rittenhouse, there was a moment when the thought entered my head: did I really see what I actually saw? As much as the trial should not have happened, at least it laid out everything to prove Rittenhouse was not some white supremacist mass shooter.

Either I'm a glutton for punishment or a workaholic (the answer is yes), but following my appearance with Tucker Carlson after I got back from the 2020 Kenosha riots, I went directly to monitor the crowds gathering outside the White House while President Trump spoke during the final night of the Republican National Convention. A large anti-Trump contingent had gathered outside.

Over the course of the evening, fights broke out between protesters and D.C. police. At one point, several Secret Service agents found themselves trapped by a hostile group outside the temporary fencing that went all along the White House and Treasury building. Once the main event was over, I saw agitators harass and physically attack RNC attendees leaving the White House, including Sen. Rand Paul (R-KY).

It had become the new normal for me—reporting on one violent event after another around the country. They simply would not stop, it seemed. Once I got home, I wondered how long this could last. It was not sustainable for me or for the country for that matter.

5

"It's Just Property, There's Insurance"

"The difference between destroying a man's livelihood and murdering him is a baby step,"—Sgt. Braxton McCoy, author of "The Glass Factory" and suicide bombing survivor.

TAKING video of burning buildings, mass looting, and general destruction of either private or government property is an easy thing to do when mass chaos breaks out. During the summer of 2020, it became a hallmark of the BLM movement riots. It certainly was a common sight I saw during my extensive travels. Whether it was Minneapolis, Kenosha, Louisville, Philadelphia, Portland, or any other town in between, there was a lot of destruction to private property.

Those particularly invested in the BLM or Antifa movements trotted out the same suite of excuses whenever I posted a video of said damage:

- There's insurance.
- It's just property.
- At least they weren't killed by a knee on their neck.
- At least they weren't shot in the back seven times.

Of course, such excuses were repeated by more than just random Twitter users. They were uttered over the airwaves of national news outlets. A book was even published about the virtues of random looting titled, forthrightly, *In Defense of Looting*.

New York Times reporter Nikole Hannah-Jones, principal author of the paper's discredited 1619 Project, was not content with being wrong on American history. She insisted on being wrong on current events, as well.

"I think we need to be very careful with our language. Yes, it is disturbing to see property being destroyed, it's disturbing to see people taking property from stores, but these are things," Hannah-Jones said. "And violence is when an agent of the state kneels on a man's neck until all of the life is leached out of his body. Destroying property, which can be replaced, is not violence. And to put those things—to use the same language to describe those two things I think really—it's not moral to do that."

In response to the first eruption of urban unrest after the death of George Floyd, longtime mainstream media commentator Sally Kohn tweeted, "I don't like violent protests, but I understand them. And those wagging their fingers against violent protests need to read up on their American history." Kohn added, "Also, and I don't feel like this should need to be pointed out, property is insured and can be replaced. Lives cannot. Check your priorities, America."

There were even reporters who criticized people like me simply for covering widespread looting in a major American city.

"Watching my Twitter feed since last night very notable the intensity of tweets from conservative voices looking to amplify/draw attention to looting in Phila. Yes it happened. NYT covered it as well. Just remarkable how conservatives want to elevate it." So tweeted Hannah-Jones's *New York Times* colleague Eric Lipton on October 28th.

The book *In Defense of Looting* was published at a very fortuitous time for author Vicky Osterweil. Coming out in August 2020, in the middle of a period when riots and urban violence held the nation's attention, the book tried to argue that looting is a victimless crime because of insurance.

As Osterweil explained to NPR, "One thing about looting is it freaks people out. But in terms of potential crimes that people can commit against the state, it's basically nonviolent. You're mass shoplifting. Most stores are insured; it's just hurting insurance companies on some level. It's just money. It's just property. It's not actually hurting any people."

The official Black Lives Matter chapter in Chicago adopted similar arguments to defend the practice in August after protesters looted and rioted following a report on social media—erroneous, as it turned out—that police had killed a black child.

"I don't care if someone decides to loot a Gucci or a Macy's or a Nike store, because that makes sure that person eats," BLM's Ariel Atkins told reporters. "That makes sure that person has clothes....That's a reparation. Anything they want to take, take it because these businesses have insurance."

I will concede I am not particularly concerned about the financial well-being of giant companies that get victimized by looters. It was hard to shed too many tears for Target Corporation when its stores were overrun in Minneapolis. (I had far more sympathy for the employees with nowhere to work when their places of employment were ransacked.)

But I'll also note that, in city after city, when the lawlessness broke out, it was often small businesses, frequently owned and run by minorities who bore the brunt of the widespread large criminality.

These are some of their stories.

MINNEAPOLIS

Names have been changed to protect the identities of those interviewed, as they wanted to remain anonymous.

The summer's chaos exacted a serious toll. After the Kenosha riots, I needed a break from covering the unrest for months on end.

So I took a week of vacation—or at least I tried to. But it turns out I'm terrible at taking a break from work. Halfway through my "vacation," I decided to stop in Minneapolis—ground zero of the 2020 unrest—to see how the city was recovering from the lawlessness it had experienced nearly four months earlier.

For the most part it had not recovered at all.

True, there were a few success stories of business owners making a comeback against the odds. But in most places, it looked as though the riots had occurred only days prior. Crime had risen to the point where I needed to hire a local private-security company as an extra set of eyes and ears while I interviewed local residents.

A sign plastered on the windows of a taco restaurant read: "We support your cause. We Support BLM. Please don't hurt our business. Thank you."

Similar signs I would spot around the city sounded more like desperate pleas, made by people being held hostage, than genuine expressions of solidarity.

My first planned stop was the Minneapolis Police 3rd Precinct.

It was still fenced off and looked to be mostly untouched since that fateful day when its officers were ordered to abandon it. The fence around the perimeter had been put up once again, and giant concrete blocks sealed off the scorched front entrance. Burn marks on the building were still very visible. Even glass that had shattered in May still lay on the ground in early September.

The rubble from the nearby liquor and tobacco store that had been burned down was gone, leaving behind an empty lot. A restaurant, which had graffiti reading "Minority Owned Business" on its window in May, was still standing. However, it was boarded up with a "Don't burn, ppl live here" sign—like a modern-day version of lamb's blood over the doorway, beseeching the angel of death to pass over a house and spare its inhabitants.

My next stop was the Cub grocery store, whose main building was still under repair. Its parking lot sported a banner reflecting its new status: "Cub Community Market." The market's temporary location, established a week after the May riots, was a tent that could only be described as a glorified farmer's market stand. Though large for a tent, it was much smaller than the Cub's main building.

An older gentleman who worked at the store said the location was still having problems with people coming by with shopping carts, emptying whole shelves of merchandise, and running out without paying. Even though store management had instructed workers not to intervene, he said he still tried to stop shoplifters whenever he could.

I headed to the GM Tobacco store, situated in a strip mall that had been targeted by rioters and looters when the mayhem grew to a fever pitch on May 27. At the time, local Minneapolis reporter Max Nesterak had filmed a group of men armed with rifles guarding GM Tobacco.

Thanks to these defenders, GM Tobacco successfully staved off attack the night of May 27. But its luck didn't last long. The store was broken into and looted early the next morning after the employees and guards had left.

Meanwhile, a sister property—another tobacco store, this one directly across from the 3rd Precinct—was looted and burned to the ground later that evening.

The stores' owners were immigrants from the Palestinian territories. In a matter of hours, they saw years of hard work destroyed to satisfy the lust for destruction of a senseless group of savage criminals.

One of the stores' owners, a man named Shawn, showed me a video of the aftermath of the GM Tobacco store that was still standing. While not nearly as trashed as the other location, it clearly would need a lot of cleanup and repair—meaning more time and money required of business owners who had sacrificed so much to build the businesses in the first place. In the video Shawn played for me, the owners walking through their damaged store had AR-15s slung across their chests.

Since the riots, the GM Tobacco owners had to spend money on not just repairs and replacement for lost inventory, but also upgrades to security. Metal bars now stretched across the store's windows and front door. Along with the AR-15s, this looked to be the new normal in the post-riot era.

The next stop was one of the main reasons for my follow-up trip. I wanted to track down "Rooftop Latinos" of Minneapolis, known to many as "Security Latinos De La Lake." I found out about the group from an NPR story detailing some of their actions during the May riots.

During the 1992 Los Angeles riots, Korean shop owners had successfully defended their livelihoods from mobs running rampant in the City of Angels. Just as we saw in Minneapolis in 2020, the riots in L.A. three decades earlier came about in the power vacuum that resulted from local police being missing in action.

The tight-knit community of Korean-American entrepreneurs and business owners in Los Angeles realized that the police weren't planning to protect them from the rampaging mob. They were going to have to do it themselves. Equipped with firearms, the shop owners posted up on their rooftops for hard cover and a superior view of the terrain. Rioters who might have looted and destroyed the Korean-Americans' businesses saw the armed defenders and, wisely, moved along. The legend of the Rooftop Koreans was born.

Fast forward to 2020. Minneapolis business owners took to their own roofs with firearms to defend themselves, their neighbors, and their livelihoods. But this time, it was the Latino community's time to shine. Their bravery—and, to be sure, their restraint—are soul-stirring illustrations of the Second Amendment's enduring importance and its central role in protecting American liberty.

I first entered a Latino grocery store on Lake Street on the city's East Side and spoke with Raul, who has run the business with his wife for several years. Raul took part in the armed watches that saved his family's business and other stores close by.

On the first day of significant violence in the city, Raul got a call around 8:30 p.m. from his cashier, urging him to come back to the store because looters were breaking into nearby businesses.

He got there as quickly as he could.

"So I tell my wife, 'Take everything that you can, take out the money from the [grocery store] safe, take all your documents. We don't know what's going to happen.' By 9:30 p.m. we rushed out with everything we could."

Safely back home, he got a call at 2:00 a.m. from the alarm company reporting a break in.

"I get into my phone to see the security cameras and, yeah, I see them coming through that window [points to the window behind him]. It wasn't many. Two kids and one lady that broke in through there with a dumbbell."

There was a counter with a cash register right by the back door. Raul said the looters grabbed that first and tried breaking into it.

"They took the whole thing and slammed it down. And it only had $100 in there. They start picking up the bills. The coins—they just dismissed them. Then they come this way [gestures to an aisle]. And they're going around and they took a shopping cart....They were grabbing stuff, putting it in [the cart]. About a half an hour later after they leave, another three come in. They come straight to that register right there. Over there they saw we had a safe."

Raul laughed about the effort the looters expended to drag the safe out the back door. Thanks to his and his wife's quick action hours earlier, the safe was empty.

"We had a bunch of phone cables, phone chargers, accessories for your phone, so [the looters] took it out. When I woke up and saw all that, I went to see my roommate downstairs, and I said, 'Hey they broke in. Should I tell my wife? I don't want her to start panicking.' They said, 'We have to because she's going to find out anyway.'"

Raul made his way back to the store in the early morning hours. No one was there. The store had weathered little real damage. Raul realized his store was lucky. Compared to businesses in areas closer to the 3rd Precinct, the vandalism at his grocery was minimal.

Raul also knew his luck was unlikely to last if he didn't take steps to protect his business.

"That night we boarded up this door," he said. "So we stayed here the rest of the night, just watching over it so that if anybody were to come, they'd know we were here, and hopefully they would just move on. We turned on all the lights and were walking back and forth."

He stayed there for ten straight nights. "That second night, I told my wife, 'We have to go just in case something happens, they throw lighter fluid or something, we're there to put it out right away.'"

Raul said when he parked his car in front of the business, he noticed the people who owned the stores across from them had gathered to protect their own side of the street. "That comforted us because I wasn't by myself."

That night there were three attempts by looters to enter his property, along with attempts to access nearby businesses. "That night we got together to talk how to proceed the next few nights, and we agreed we would be outside or inside our businesses," Raul told me. "Two of them were going to get security, by that I mean people with weapons, not an actual security company. So the following night, we had about six people with weapons. From that point, two were upstairs with me on the roof, two were [on the other roof]. And then we were just watching over each corner of the block."

Raul said another armed group from a nearby neighborhood approached his own to offer backup if needed.

"We did have about six to ten people from the neighborhood in each building that came to help us...So I guess there were about 18 to 20 people in total" to protect the intersection where the stores were located.

Their arms were largely handguns and rifles, such as AR-15s, which Raul attested were essential in protecting their small part of Minneapolis when all else failed.

"This [business] is my wife's future, this is our future. We were here to not be violent, but to at least try to protect as much as we could...I came into my wife's life six years ago, and I've been helping her run the business. For me it's like I need to be there for her. I need to help her get this going forward and not just let anybody come in and destroy it. It was just a safety matter...we felt more secure."

The Rooftop Latinos were largely successful in protecting their livelihoods. But they weren't the only ones who had to take matters into their own hands.

Just down the street in the opposite direction from the 3rd Precinct, rioters zeroed in on a strip mall with a vulnerable row of businesses.

One of those businesses is owned by a woman named Jessica, who lives above her shop. She was watching the live feeds showing the mob heading in her direction.

One of her employees, on his own initiative, parked across the street to monitor the outside of the store. Around midnight, he called to tell her he saw someone pick up a rock and throw it through the front window of the next-door business. Another rioter smashed a baseball bat through other windows. People rushed through the breaches to pillage and loot.

A Walgreens a block away was set on fire. Jessica's concern for her safety and for her shop was through the roof.

"I thought I was dead," she said. "I am not a panicky person; I am not a person who gets excited easily, but this was a whole new deal. I called 911, no answer. So I called my brother...I said, 'I just wanted to call you, I don't want to call Mom and Dad, but if I'm not here in the morning, I love you.'"

Jessica is physically disabled. She was increasingly worried about being able to evacuate quickly if her store caught on fire.

"I mean I was just frightened. I had my dogs on leashes, I had my purse, my driver's license, passport, and my birth certificate, and a pair of underwear."

One of her employees, Harold, has a conceal carry permit. He decided to come and help protect the store after midnight. Because Jessica's brother is friends with a county sheriff in northern Minnesota, they were able to get ahold of the Hennepin County Sheriff's Office. The Sheriff's Office was then able to call Jessica and keep her on the line while a second employee drove to the store.

The Sheriff's Office advised them to hunker down and not leave the store unless absolutely necessary. The two of them stayed up all night, with Harold making security rounds on the roof every couple of minutes.

In the aftermath of the May 27 destruction, Harold said, Jessica realized she would have to pay for a private security company to protect her store—and her life—at considerable expense.

Harold said that, "all these businesses that we know were everyday people. For the most part, these were not rich-owned private corporations, these are just regular everyday people that were already struggling because of COVID, because of the restrictions there, and [they] lost their livelihoods."

He continued, saying, "I've been so frustrated time and time again when people say, 'Well, they're just buildings. It'll be fine.' And it's like no, I mean, a lot of these people were underinsured, though no fault of their own."

Harold pointed out that the city government, at least at first, was not giving demolition permits to the owners of destroyed businesses because they were still on the hook for the second half of their property taxes. But many were unable to pay due to poor business resulting from COVID restrictions.

"I think it's been such a shame that people don't talk about the humanity of these [business owners]," he said. "They weren't just buildings. These were normal people who lost their livelihoods."

If rioters had managed to destroy Jessica's store, at least two-dozen families who rely on her business being operational would have been completely out of luck.

"I have 25 families that depend on me to be in business, and I work hard to do that. And it could have been gone in a match light."

She added, "Everybody has the right to protest. But the moment that changes from a protest to someone breaking a window, you become a criminal. And no one has the right to be a criminal."

Even before the Minneapolis Police Department's involvement in the death of George Floyd, previous department controversies had spurred local activists to defund—and even totally abolish—the police force.

Those calls had never sat well with business owners.

"I do not agree with defunding the police department at all. I do think there needs to be change," Jessica said. "If you want to take the department and don't want to call them the 'police' anymore, that's fine," she said.

Referring to the grandstanding by the Minneapolis City Council, she added, "But you can't defund the police and not have a plan in place."

GM Tobacco's co-owner, Shawn, echoed that sentiment, saying he was convinced immigrant and minority communities would be hurt the most if the police department were abolished. "I really can't imagine the town without police. It would be bad."

It's hardly a surprise that when the city council voted to eliminate the police department, and in the middle of a crime surge to boot, quite a few business owners decided to pack up and leave town.

One man I interviewed, Aaron, sold his business after owning it for 25 years.

Aaron's family-run store, located near the 3rd Precinct, was broken into during the May riots. While he was able to reopen a few days once things calmed down, it was never the same. The boards covering busted-out windows stayed up for months because the glass companies were so overwhelmed and backlogged with orders.

"I served in the military, but I never was in any battles and wars or anything like that so I've never experienced PTSD, but this has got to be close," said Aaron. "Afterwards, I was just constantly looking for my phone to go off, alarm company calling me, it was months and months and months of almost on pins and needles, just thinking, 'Is something else going to happen?' It wasn't anything I ever experienced before in my life."

Aaron's decision to close his shop did not happen right after the chaos subsided.

"I told [my family], 'I'm going to give Minneapolis all summer long to figure this thing out and, obviously, provide protection for the city, residents, businesses, and if they don't then we'll start talking.' And sure enough they didn't. It actually got worse because they started to take more and more funding from the police....We didn't feel safe anymore. We decided to change our hours to only be open when it was light out."

Aaron said he still agonized over selling the store but was ultimately "forced out because [the city] wouldn't provide protection anymore." Aaron said he was far from the only business owner who wanted to leave the Twin Cities.

"There are quite a few that have told me, 'I am thinking about selling,'" he pointed out. "There's another one that I was talking to when he found out we were closing down, and he said, 'If I could sell my place, I'd be gone too.' There's a lot of businesses that are not feeling safe in Minneapolis anymore."

Since my interviews, which took place amid a surge in crime, some city council members tried walking back their votes to get rid of the MPD.

My interviews also took place shortly after a subsequent bout of civic unrest in Minneapolis. Those riots came in reaction to a rumor, spread largely through social media, that MPD officers had killed another black man. The individual actually committed suicide. But the damage—another orgy of destruction and vandalism—was already done by the time the truth came out.

In turn, a number of Minneapolis residents are now primed to confront mobs whether or not an injustice has actually occurred. Jessica and other owners of nearby stores have banded together to create the East Lake Street Business Watch Patrol.

"The idea is to have someone available to patrol the neighborhood to keep a close eye on our properties late at night as needed," said Jessica. "The expectation is only for another set of eyes looking for things out of place or suspicious activity. If the patrol sees something, a phone call would be made to the business owner and that business owner would take it from there."

Many business owners personally affected by the riots obviously felt what happened to them was wrong.

Surprisingly, though, not everyone.

When Twin Cities restaurant Gandhi Mahal was destroyed by arson during the riots, the daughter of owner Ruhel Islam, a Bangladeshi immigrant, wrote on the restaurant's Facebook page that the family sided with protesters. In a post that went viral, Hafsa Islam said she heard her father tell someone on the phone, "Let my building burn. Justice needs to be served; put those officers in jail."

Hafsa continued: "Gandhi Mahal may have felt the flames last night, but our fiery drive to help protect and stand with our community will never die! Peace be with everyone. #JusticeforGeorgeFloyd #BLM."

The Islams started another, smaller restaurant two miles away called Curry in a Hurry. In an ironic footnote, in July 2021, the restaurant's van, filed with catering supplies and other kitchen gear, was stolen outside the family's home. Islam asked for his followers on social media to call the police if they spotted the van.*

NEW YORK CITY

Bronx Optical Center had been closed for around three months due to the COVID-19 lockdowns. It was finally allowed to open in May since it was considered to be an essential business, but the eye care center was not spared when riots broke out on June 1. Jessica Betancourt, the owner and vice president of the BJT Bronx Merchant Association, said the cost of repairs and loss in merchandise totaled around $200,000. After being open for only a few weeks, it had to close down once again for 28 days. Almost two years later, Betancourt told me while the items have been replaced and the store was repaired, she and her employees are still emotionally scarred by what happened.

"Anybody can just get up and move on, but it's a hit mentally because we were in shock being looted. Yes, we have insurance; we can pick up and move on, but that can never be forgotten," she said. "We have it inside ourselves, 'Oh it can happen again' because the looters know they're not going to be penalized for anything."

In the Bronx, 118 arrests related to the riots were made in June, but the Bronx District Attorney and the courts dismissed 73 of them, leav-

---

* Kyle Hooten, "Pro-riot business owner now wants police to find his stolen van," Alpha News, July 23, 2021.

ing just 18 cases open. While there have been 19 convictions, those were mostly lesser offenses such as trespassing, which carry no jail time.

Betancourt said the charges being dropped was "disgusting," and it showed how the city turned their backs towards the small business owners who were victims of the lawlessness while giving the green light to would-be robbers.

Unlike a lot of businesses that were looted and damaged, Betancourt noted they provide crucial medical services to members of the local community, which they were denied for nearly a month because of the rioters' actions.

"In the back of my mind, they can do it again. I have not forgotten... We serve everyone and we don't stereotype; we treat everybody the same, but in the back of our heads, it can happen again."

KENOSHA

I returned to Kenosha multiple times after the riots, taking note how the city slowly changed from December 2020 to July 2021. When I traveled to Kenosha with my good friend Chase in December, four months after the riots sparked by the Jacob Blake shooting, I joked how there were fewer fires this time around.

Like Minneapolis, the hard-hit areas of Kenosha looked little different from when I had left in late August. Windows on businesses remained boarded up, often covered with graffiti reading "BLM" or "Justice for [insert name]." Rubble and debris filled lots where, as recently as that summer, buildings once stood. The businesses that were right on the hardest hit streets had other messages: "Animals Inside." One of the only real differences I noticed was the layer of snow atop the rubble.

We visited the 63rd Street location of one of the more horrific scenes of violence and destruction back in August. The Danish Brotherhood Lodge Hall had been there since 1910. In a matter of hours, a century's worth of its history had gone up in flames. Also destroyed was the ground-floor business, The Mattress Shop, which had been located there since 2009.

In a grotesque scene caught on camera, an elderly man named Robert Cobb, a member of the Danish Brotherhood Lodge and employee of the mattress store, was shown trying to deter rioters and looters with a fire extinguisher. Video captured someone running up behind him and viciously hitting Cobb in the head with a Gatorade bottle filled with con-crete. The blow knocked him unconscious and broke his jaw.

Chase and I surveyed the burned-out building, which was now sec-tioned off with a chain-linked fence. A sign gave the address of the Mat-tress Shop's new location. We went to the new store, further away from downtown, and talked with both Cobb and owner Pamela Moniz about the aftermath.[39]

"It was devastating," said Pamela, fighting tears. "It was years and years of memories and our livelihood and that was home, that was home to a lot of people in that neighborhood."

She talked a bit about the challenges that many businesses faced trying to recover from the nights of anarchy that laid waste to Kenosha.

"A lot of insurance companies were fighting insurance claims. A lot of people didn't have the proper coverage. A lot of small businesses, mom-and-pop places, sunk. They were already battling the pandemic...and then this. You know, it's a lot of financial hurdles. After that happened, finding real estate [was a hurdle] because a lot of other places were look-ing for new homes."

I then asked Pamela how she felt about people's "It's just property" excuse.

She scoffed. "It's not just property," she said. "It's not just property and especially [Robert], he's not just property."

"I don't know how anybody can say that," Robert chimed in. "I go by there every day; I went by there this morning, every day I go by there—thinking, hoping, something [changes]...It was just more than a place of business. I belonged to the Brotherhood, which was upstairs. On Friday nights, I played cards, I played bingo or whatever. I don't drink, I don't smoke, but I do want to get out, I want to do something."

"That was home," Pamela added, then showed me a Facebook post from a friend with pictures of the store in flames. Accompanying the post was this commentary:

"It wasn't just a mattress shop that those pieces of shit lit on fire, it wasn't just some random guy that they jumped and broke his jaw when he attempted to put it out. It was a shop that many in the neighborhood frequented for the sense of belonging, a place where friends gathered for the good times and bad. And that man would quite literally give you the shirt off his back, was ALWAYS helping somebody out, and often giving way more than he should. He didn't care who you were, where you came from, what your story was, if he had the means to lighten your load, he absolutely would. I'm just heartbroken for my great friends. I don't have words. There is no justification for this. There is no point. It's terrorism, plain and simple. It wasn't just a fucking mattress shop."

Pamela thought of the broader implications of what they had gone through in Kenosha. "It can happen anywhere at any time to anybody.

Kenosha is the last place that people would have thought something like this could have happened." Still, she added, people shouldn't give up in the face of such adversity or stop spreading kindness, no matter how hard it may seem.

They also wanted to make clear they believed no one from their part of town took part in the destruction. People who lived elsewhere almost certainly conducted it.

"The night after my store burned, and there were rumors of [rioters] going into the residential areas and burning, you know, this is days of not sleeping, this is days of just being on edge, listening to the [police] scanner and having live feeds," Pamela said. "We packed up; we packed up all our dogs and all our cats and went out of [the] county because we couldn't even sleep in our homes."

I first met Scott Carpenter and his mother, Linda, whom I wrote about in Chapter 4, the day after Kenosha experienced its second night of unrest. The Carpenters' emotions were still raw watching the remains of their family-owned business, B&L Office Furniture Inc., still smoldering the morning after.

I followed up with Scott in February to see how he and his family were doing. He was one of the lucky ones to still have an operation going, albeit at a new location. They were still in Kenosha, but now comfortably outside downtown.

Scott said they tried to open as soon as they could. They were losing too much business while closed.

"We move forward, we're doing okay," Scott explained. "Probably within a month and a half or so we found ourselves a place to open. We owned the building we were in and to rebuild would have been over a million dollars."

Scott was among the business owners then-President Trump met with when he visited Kenosha shortly after order was restored. He said he understood Trump's trip was a bit of a "dog and pony show," but it was still "pretty cool" and an "interesting" event to be a part of.

"It was totally something different; and it was nice the thought was there, the good intent," Scott said. But the money Trump mentioned he was going to get for the affected business owners "never came."

Scott said in the months after the riots, Kenosha had become "slow," with businesses still having boards up for weeks afterward."

According to Scott, the riots gave the town something of a stigma. "People were afraid to come into Kenosha," he said. "I had friends that lived west of Kenosha, and they are like, 'I'm not coming into town. It's just dangerous.' I'm like, 'It is not! There's no danger, there's no fear.'"

Scott then detailed some of the challenges he and others faced trying to rebuild their livelihoods.

"Everybody was pretty much left on their own, and the city didn't do anything to help anybody out, that I'm aware of. They didn't give us any grace of any kind on anything. You know even for like our property taxes; you would think, ok, you pay your property tax based on what? What you have. Well, this was taken from us; you'd think [they] would prorate this, right? And they're like, 'No.'"

The loss of B&L's original location forced Scott to significantly change how they run the business. They went from 10,000 square feet of space to 4,000. But Scott remains positive. "We'll make do with it. I'm pretty optimistic about it."

Scott, who has lived in and around Kenosha his entire life, said he wants people to know the town is friendly.

"We welcome outsiders in. We're not a stuck-up town, we're not up-pity, we don't feel like we're too good for other people. We want people to come, and we want to welcome them." Most importantly, he said, "We want people to know we're still in business. You know, it's a cool little place."

Right down the street from B&L Office Furniture's old location is Ed's Used Tires. I met owner Linda Tolliver on one trip to Wisconsin in June 2021. I noticed how the boards that were up in December were no longer there.

Linda told me she had been out to lunch with her family on August 23rd when she saw the Blake video. Right away, she knew things were headed out of control.

"The fact that the Mayor and the Governor didn't see fit to get the National Guard here as quickly as possible is what I think caused a lot of what happened," she said. "I think the National Guard could have prevented a lot; there was still going to be some rioting and definitely some peaceful protesting, but it wouldn't have turned into as bad as it did."

Her business, which has been in Kenosha since 1961, sustained around $25,000 in damage:

- Half the store's windows were broken
- The front door was broken in
- A safe was stolen
- An ATM was stolen
- The register was "busted"
- Statues out front of her shop were broken, with the heads broken off "so [rioters] could throw them through other people's windows."
- A wooden church bench she had outside was thrown through the front of the shop: "When I got here it was scorched, so somebody had tried to light it on fire, but it didn't catch."

Linda recalled coming to the store within minutes of the vandalism taking place. She lives close by and saw the damage over livestreams. As she drove in, other people watching the livestream told her a "Good Samaritan" was standing outside the place trying to ward people off.

"I was pretty much in shock," Linda said, adding how worried she was because B&L Office Furniture was completely engulfed in flames by the time she arrived.

"The heat was intense. There was orange smoke everywhere. The power went out; they had to shut down the power. I ended up staying the night here. I had the SWAT team on one side of me [and] the fire department on the other side of me. I just didn't feel comfortable leaving with no windows. I mean, they didn't steal absolutely everything but if I left, I'm afraid they would have."

One of Linda's biggest concerns was the large number of tires in her shop if it became a raging inferno. That would have posed significant dangers for the houses nearby. She was also concerned for the safety of her pet birds.

At daylight, she boarded up the store and closed for around aweek-and-a-half. That "cost me a lot because I'm a paycheck-to-paycheck kind of business. It's a small business and when I'm out a week's worth of revenue, it affects me in a major way. It almost killed [the business]. I've gone through a lot of different things; this almost took me down."

At the time of the interview, almost a year later, Linda said she was still waiting to hear back if she would be given a grant from the city. When it came to people dismissing her plight because all that happened to her was property damage, Linda shook her head.

"These people have no idea how insurance works. They probably don't even have car insurance. They don't understand things like deductibles and if you have house insurance, there's certain things that are not going to be covered in your house," she said. "My insurance did not cover [everything]. They covered $2,000 total. They covered the stupid broken [statues], as if I need the statues to run my business."

I noticed the car lot that had been next to Ed's Used Tires was now empty. Linda said the owner moved his business out of town.

Right across the street from Ed's Used Tires is Treasures Within, which was also heavily targeted by looters on the night of August 24th. Jim Degrazio, the owner of the thrift store, told the *Milwaukee Journal Sentinel* during the August riots that his business sustained at least $10,000 worth in damage, which included an attempted arson. Those costs were in addition to the untold amount of merchandise that was stolen. Jim said the security cameras caught people stealing "armfuls" of items from the store.

"I actually came down here because I had a friend that was out front that lives in the building next door," Jim told me. The friend told him "the windows were gone but they were starting a fire…They started two fires in here. It was terrible, you know—my reaction was why? Why us? Why me? I didn't do anything to anybody."

The store's security cameras captured everything, including the attempts to set fire to the building. Jim turned over the video to the Bureau of Alcohol, Tobacco, Firearms and Explosives.

"Our insurance didn't cover anything. It's called domestic terrorism," he said. "They covered nothing out of all the stuff that was taken."

Jim had strong words when I asked him how he felt about the "it's just property" argument.

"Well, that's probably one of the most untrue statements I've ever heard. I mean some people say that if you try to protect your property, you care about your property more than their life and if they're in here stealing, they're obviously thinking my property is more important than their life."

Jim continued: "I think the whole situation was bad...There's businesses like myself; we didn't do anything to anybody. If you have a problem with somebody or something, if you're going to target, target wherever your problem is. I'm not saying target it, but if you're going to target something, go after where the problem originated. Why mess with the people that serve the community?"

Jim said it took him three months to fully reopen after the riots, but it will take "years" for the business to fully recover.

Even when people were arrested and charged for the destruction, it did not necessarily mean relief or peace for the victims.

On July 13th, 2021, the U.S. Attorney's Office for the Eastern District of Wisconsin announced it had charged four men, in two separate cases, for various offenses during the Kenosha riots. One of the men, Devon Vaughn, was charged with arson in relation to the fire at B&L Office Furniture.[40]

I asked Scott Carpenter how it felt that at least one person might be brought to justice for destroying the location of his family's business.

"To be honest with you, it really doesn't mean a whole lot," he told me. "It's not like it will undo anything that was done or make anything

better. But I am curious to know about the persons' involved background. What or why would they think that this would help with civil rights? Or was this done in hopes to create a civil war inside of our town? Or was it just thoughtlessness—destructive behavior done for no reason at all? The people I saw in the pictures did not look like five-year-olds playing with matches. These were adults that knew better than what they did."

He added he was "more discouraged about our government leaders allowing stuff like this to happen inside of our country."

At their new location, Scott keeps a vase that was inside the original location when it was burned down. It was one of the only items they were able to save. Now it sits by his desk, still charred with a little bit of ash inside, as a reminder of what happened.

KENOSHA AFTERMATH

In total, the cost of the riots to this medium-size town was immense.

The *Kenosha News* reported in September that the Kenosha Area Business Alliance estimated the costs at $50 million.

But dollar figures are impersonal. They don't reflect the lives and livelihoods ruined, or the despair and anguish suffered by so many innocent people. Nor do they capture the sense that life in a community like Kenosha had changed forever, and not in a good way.

Fifty million dollars is a huge amount of money. To my mind, however, a more revealing number to describe the cost of the riots to the community is 40. That is how many businesses in Kenosha ended up closed for good because of the city's several days of unrest during the summer of 2020.

Those who I spoke to that still lived and worked in the immediate area were concerned about the outcome of the legal cases involving Rittenhouse, Blake, and Officer Rusten Sheskey, the officer whose shooting of Blake touched off the Kenosha riots. They had doubts about state or local authorities being able to prevent further destruction if there is anger over verdicts in certain cases.

The whole city held its breath as the Kenosha County District Attorney prepared to announce whether to charge Sheskey. Fencing was put back up around the county courthouse. The Wisconsin National Guard were activated. Finally, on January 5th, the DA said he would *not* be charging Sheskey for any wrongdoing. There were small protests in Kenosha following the announcement, but I truly believe the town was spared additional riots because it was the dead of winter. You could almost sense the city exhale.

When the announcement came, I was already headed to my next assignment: Washington, DC. Just two weeks before Joe Biden's scheduled inauguration as the nation's 46th president, a pro-Trump protest was planned for January 6th.

What a day *that* would turn out to be.

6

"January 6th Was Worse Than 9/11"

LET'S state the obvious to get it out of the way: The Capitol riot that happened on January 6th, 2021, was wrong and should not have happened, just like the other riots I covered. That said, it's no surprise some people want to take what happened and use it to suit their political objectives.

This is my account of what occurred that day.

"So I'll be Metroing down to DC in a bit. Plan is to get the peaceful Trump supporters during the day and then [the] fights at night." That's the message I sent my boss over GChat the morning of January 6th.

The reason I was confident about how the day would unfold was because the previous two pro-Trump marches and rallies in Washington, DC, after the election had played out that way. I fully expected January 6, 2021, to reprise the events of those days.

On November 14th, I had arrived at BLM Plaza just in time to get video of individual and small groups of Trump supporters being attacked by Antifa and Black Lives Matter rioters. BLM Plaza was the name the District of Columbia government had given that summer to the two-block stretch of 16th St., right by Lafayette and the White House in northwest Washington.

Patrons eating outside at P.J. Clarke's restaurant were swarmed.

Protesters hurled projectiles and shot fireworks at them. Victims fled or ran inside for cover.

The initial police response was slow. Rioters took advantage of this to brazenly stroll around searching for more Trump supporters to attack.

One group of rioters tried to enter the lobby of a hotel near the White House after seeing Trump supporters emerge. But local police, spurred to action, made a mad dash to cut them off and prevent the rioters from going inside. Unable to enter the hotel, Antifa and BLM protesters taunted the Trump supporters huddling in the lobby. They set on fire the pro-Trump merchandise they had stolen and vandalized a pickup truck parked in front of the hotel. Someone slashed the truck's tires, the air hissing loudly as it escaped.

Once the hotel was secured, the group wandered away, with police officers following on bicycles. The mob harassed Trump supporters eating at the Willard Hotel's restaurant. They looted a merchandise stand run by a black man that was selling pro-Trump merchandise, hoping to set its contents on fire.

District of Columbia police officers finally moved in to push the group out and contain the fires. About the same time, a larger group of Proud Boys arrived, intent on fighting the Antifa and BLM protesters.

Most ran off, with a few holding back to face off with the Proud Boys. Combatants used pepper spray, including bear mace.

Police surged closer, arresting people from both groups while attempting to separate them and prevent further fighting.

When it became clear police were not going to let the two groups fight, the Proud Boys headed in one direction, and the Antifa/BLM group left in another. That ended the violence, at least for that night.

It was much the same when another "Stop the Steal" march took place on December 12th. This time, however, far more Proud Boys showed up. The massive increase in attendance from Proud Boys, decked out in their black and gold "uniforms," was spurred by the abject failure of police during the November riots to keep Trump supporters safe. The Proud Boys were hoping the same shooting-fish-in-a-barrel atmosphere they encountered in November would prevail in December.

Those hopes were dashed. Seeking to avoid a repeat of the November debacle, DC police and the U.S. Park Police showed up in full force. The increased police presence helped keep the two sides separate, by and large. Crisis averted...for the time being.

I spent most of the day on January 5th near the White House. A few skirmishes broke out by BLM Plaza, but police did a commendable job keeping would-be combatants apart.

Interestingly, the pro-Trump crowd often became enraged with police for keeping them from getting face-to-face with the Antifa and BLM protesters. Some accused the police of being "traitors" for protecting "domestic terrorists."

In retrospect, what was notable was the feistiness of Trump supporters and their willingness to mix it up both with protesters and with police. Looking back, it was a red flag that I (and many others) missed given what was to come 24 hours later.

I expected January 6th to play out like the day before: peaceful during the day, perhaps some fighting at night.

Despite my desire to not carry all of my riot gear with me until dark, I still put it on when I left home that morning. I knew I probably wouldn't have time to go back home to grab it once the need for it arose. It was a smart decision.

I arrived at the Washington Monument around 11:20 a.m. The pro-Trump crowd numbered in the thousands and was growing by the minute, all waiting to hear President Trump speak. The scene was calm. Nobody in the crowd seemed antagonistic towards the police officers around the Ellipse. I took a sweeping video to show the crowd size. Due to the volume of people using the cell network, I was unable to upload it on Twitter, much less get a signal. I started walking towards the White House hoping for better luck to get the video up.

As I approached Lafayette Square, my friend Kaylee Beal, who was a Daily Caller reporter at the time, texted me, "Everyone going to [Capitol Hill]." It was 12:25 p.m. The distance from the White House to the Capitol building is a bit of walk, especially with all my gear on. To save time, and my legs, I went to Farragut West Metro Station and took the subway to the Capitol South Station.

Exiting the Metro, I immediately sensed something was off. Police were blocking peoples' ability to go north on First Street, which runs right by the Cannon House Office Building directly on the way to the Capitol. I circled around several blocks to South Capitol St, which runs along the

Rayburn House Office Building, which by the way is the worst-designed Congressional office building.

Approaching the Capitol grounds, I could hear shouting and the sound of metal banging. I started to run closer when I saw a huge crowd making its way onto the grounds on the west side of the Capitol building. I hopped onto one of the small risers that had been built for the upcoming Inauguration to film video of the swarming crowd. Unlike the calm at the White House, there was an ominous feeling in the air at the Capitol. Some in the crowd were ripping the short, temporary fencing away to allow more people onto the grounds.

"Oh, so it's going to be that kind of day."

I could see a small number of Capitol police officers climbing onto the still-unfinished Inauguration Day platform, intent on making a stand there. The officers were not in riot gear and were vastly outnumbered.

Here I witnessed something I'd seen many other times before in places like Minneapolis, Portland, and Seattle: the moment when a crowd begins to transform from protesters into rioters.

What made January 6th different were the people who made up the crowd. The protests and riots in the wake of George Floyd's murder and the shooting of Jacob Blake were constituted largely by people, it's fair to say, with no great affection for the police, for capitalism, or for Donald Trump. This crowd was made up of people who, it's fair to say, regarded the protesters and rioters of 2020 with contempt—people who thought authorities had not done nearly enough to stop the destruction and devastation that plagued so many American cities.

It was as if roles had been switched.

Some in the crowd threw projectiles at officers. Others directed pepper spray at police, resulting in several officers coming off the line. This was bad news; police were short-staffed and needed everybody they could muster to hold the defensive line.

Clashes between the two sides flared constantly. A white man next to me threw up a Nazi salute towards the police. Another man walked around handing out small rocks for people to throw. A few Trump supporters made their way up the Inauguration-platform scaffolding, with officers chasing close behind.

Officers used every weapon in their arsenal—pepper spray, tear gas, flashbangs, and pepper balls—shy of firing their guns. I was hit directly in the left hand and upper right bicep with pepper balls.

When I took my ballistic helmet off and placed it on a ledge to put on my gas mask, a man grabbed my helmet and raised it above his head as if to lead the mob that had assembled. I yanked his arm down to get my helmet back.

Police in riot gear arrived and began to push the crowd back with heavy-duty pepper spray canisters. I noticed a large smattering of blood pooling on the ground, but was unable to determine whose it was.

"This is our building!" one man yelled at the officers. "This is our country! You guys are on the side of treason."

"You should be mad too!" a woman screamed.

Officers established a defensive line close to a set of steps leading up to the Capitol. One protester rushed forward, pushing and kicking some of the police. A few officers hit back and used pepper spray on the surging crowd. However, many law enforcement officers were not wearing gas masks. Their vulnerability was exposed when one rioter used his own mace on police.

"Get me some people up on this line!" a Capitol Police sergeant shouted after a handful of officers fell out.

The fighting stopped for a few minutes once the police line stabilized. I walked away from the Capitol building to try to upload videos since, once again, the growing crowd resulted in poor cell data.

The further I walked away from the Capitol, the calmer things got. Walking north towards Union Station, Trump supporters who were not at the riot were milling about and wondering out loud what was happening. Others had been at or near the Capitol but were leaving so as not to be a part of what the day was turning into.

The only thing that signified anything was wrong was the constant noise of police sirens. By the time I returned to the Capitol, the law enforcement defensive line on the west side of the building had collapsed. The rioters who wanted to brawl had simply outnumbered the officers.

On the lawn close to the Senate chamber side, I saw rioters chasing away a small group of riot police officers. Several Trump supporters tried to get the crowd to stop chasing them and to stop throwing things, but they too were outnumbered and were unsuccessful.

The only thing police could do was to fall back to the east side of the Capitol facing the Supreme Court—the other side from where the mobs initially had been gathering—to regroup with reinforcements. They were chased the whole way by rioters.

The rioters were temporarily stopped at the steps near the Senate chamber. But once the crowd became big enough, they pushed both barriers and officers aside.

By this time, the inside of the Capitol had already been breached.

The east side steps that lead directly into the Rotunda were filled with people. Others were trying to break windows on the ground floor. Attempts to enter the doors that are underneath the Senate steps failed after officers were able to secure the doorways.

I was still outside trying to figure where to go next when I saw on Twitter that not only had the Capitol been breached in multiple places, but also someone had been shot.

"Well now I really need to get inside."

I made my way up the steps that lead into the Rotunda. The main door was open, with people pushing hard to get in. A few officers tried to stop them, with one almost losing control of his riot shield after some in the crowd grabbed it. Despite the officers' best attempts, the crowd was able to squeeze their way inside. Two officers in the main doorway could do nothing but stand off to the side.

The situation in the Rotunda, while tense, was calmer. Officers stood around unsure of what to do. Many of the people who had rushed inside were looking around and, I assume, taking in the view. One man was using an old flip phone to take photos.

Closer to the hallway that leads to Speaker Nancy Pelosi's office, officers made a defensive line, preventing people from going further into the complex. A few minutes later, police rushed into the Rotunda to push everyone out the same doorway they had come in. Since rioters were at first resisting the police's efforts, pepper spray was being used once again. I threw on my gas mask for the third time that day.

"If you don't fucking stop, I'm leaving your ass here!" a woman was telling either her husband or boyfriend. "I'm telling you, look at me in my eyes! Look in my fucking eyes! If you don't stop, I'm leaving your ass here!"

I soon realized the dangerous situation I had put myself in. The doorway that leads to the outside, much like most of the Capitol's doorways, is very narrow. Everyone was starting to be packed really tight against each other with nowhere to go. Those outside the building trying to get in couldn't see that we were being pushed out by the police. People were

Minneapolis, May 28th: Inside the looted Target.

Minneapolis, May 28th: Burned out building and vehicle down the street from the 3rd Precinct.

Minneapolis, May 28th:
Workers putting boards
on the liquor store across
the street from the 3rd
Precinct. It would later
be broken into and set
on fire.

Minneapolis, May 28th:
Looters attempting to break
into an ATM machine inside
Cub Foods.

**Minneapolis, May
28th:** Moments after
rioters tore down some
of the fencing around
the 3rd Precinct.

Minneapolis, May 28th: Rioters set fire to a mobile light tower in the motor pool of the 3rd Precinct after MPD officers were ordered to evacuate. (*left*)

Minneapolis, May 28th: Rioters celebrating in front of the burning 3rd Precinct. The liquor store across the street is also on fire. (*below*)

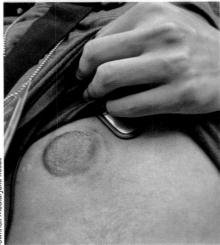

Minneapolis, May 29th: Rubber bullet wound about ten minutes after I was hit in the stomach area just below the ribs. I still have a scar to this day. (*left*)

Minneapolis, May 29th: MN State Police guarding burnt-out buildings.

Seattle, June 9th: The outside of SPD's East Precinct after it was evacuated.

Seattle, June 9th: The outside of SPD's East Precinct after it was evacuated. (*left*)

Seattle, July 1st: The outside of SPD's East Precinct after officers moved in. (*below*)

Kenosha, August 24th: Kenosha County Democrats' office boarded up after riots broke out on August 23rd. (*left*)

Kenosha, August 24th: One of the many city garbage trucks that were set on fire near the Kenosha County Courthouse.

Kenosha, August 24th: Sheriff's deputies establish a perimeter near the burning B&L Office Furniture building so firefighters could safely respond.

Minneapolis, September 3rd: Businesses that survived the chaos in May were still boarded up months later.

Minneapolis, September 3rd: One of the U.S. Postal Service's office that was burned in May.

Minneapolis, September 3rd: More pleas from business owners for rioters to not attack them.

Wauwatosa, October 8th: The inside of a home that were damaged after rioters attacked multiple buildings on October 7th. The resident was home when it was attacked.

Kenosha, December 13th: Many businesses that were burned down in August remained untouched.

Kenosha, December 13th: The burned-out wreckage of stores that had apartment units above. (*above*)

Washington, D.C., January 6th: Capitol and city police form a defensive line after Trump supporters tried to storm the west side of the Capitol building. The line would eventually be breached due to the large crowd pushing forward. (*right*)

falling on top of each other, and some were trampled. I knew that if I fell, I would have a hard time getting back up.

As I got closer to the police line, I flashed my Capitol press credentials in the hopes the officers would let me through to the other side. It almost worked. The first officer passed me off to another closer to their side of the single line they had made. It went on until I was almost through, but the last officer I had to get by pushed me back into the increasingly panicking crowd.

"We can't move, you fucking idiots!" one woman screamed at police. "We can't go any further! We can't go any further!"

I found myself in front of one officer who, seeing I was press and not fighting them, grabbed on to my ballistic vest. I could barely hear him over the roaring din, but made out that he said he would hold onto me. He told me to put my phone away so I wouldn't drop it. I grabbed onto his wrist to ensure I wouldn't lose him. I started to calm down for a second until another officer came up behind him and pushed me away. He had no choice but to let go.

Once more I found myself in the crush of the crowd. I knew there was a bench nearby in the corridor off to the side, just a few feet away. I hoped to make my way there and stand on it above the crowd. I did make it, only to find people were sitting down on it. They were trying to get up but kept being pushed down by the packed crowd.

It was getting very difficult to breathe. My vest, which had kept me safe during all the gunfire I'd found myself in during other riots, was now helping to suffocate me as its rifle plates were pushed against my chest from the crush of people pushing into me. It got to the point where I truly thought I might suffocate and die right inside the United States Capitol.

I somehow was able to inch my way closer to the doorway. Once there, I locked eyes with a man who was nearby and screamed, "PULL ME OUT!"

"WHAT?"

"PULL ME OUT!"

The man grabbed my ballistic vest and yanked me out. I give him credit for saving my life.

I was angry once I got outside—angry at what the rioters were doing.

Not only was what they were doing wrong, but all of the past riots I had covered no longer mattered on the national level.

Before, Democrats and those in the mainstream media would try to minimize the reality of the riots that had hit Main Street in 2020 because of who was committing them.

With the assault on the Capitol, Democrats and their allies now would be able to dismiss the past (and future) riots perpetrated by people to whom they are sympathetic with this simple argument: "Look what Trump supporters did."

Besides the White House or the Supreme Court, you can't do worse than attacking the building that houses one of the branches of the U.S. government.

And for what?

The people who breached the Capitol not only failed to achieve their goal of stopping the election certification process, they gave their political opponents exactly what they wanted after a year of BLM-related unrest: Trump supporters rioting.

I kicked myself out of my self-pity once I linked up with Kaylee. We had been trying to find each other since the start of the day but had a hard time because of the poor cell phone service. The two of us walked over to the north side of the Capitol where rioters were still fighting with the police. In one side entrance, rioters were continuing to try to break in.

One man had grabbed a metal rack, tied a "Drain the Swamp" flag to it, and rammed it repeatedly against the door. He didn't realize the door opened outwards, so his efforts achieved nothing. Between blows, officers inside cracked the door open and unleashed a thick cloud of CS powder, a riot-control agent that is the defining component of tear gas. It was thick enough to cloud the whole entranceway to near zero visibility. The dust coated my gear in a fine white powder that would take weeks to clean off. Using the cloud as cover, officers with gas masks on poured out and started pushing people back from the entrance.

The outside hallway leading to that entrance is very narrow. Police in full riot gear were using shields to physically shove rioters back. Wanting to get video of the action, I climbed on top of a wide ledge that gave me a good overhead view. When the officers got to where another reporter and I were, they threatened to turn their batons on us to get us down.

Unsatisfied at how slowly we were moving, one officer grabbed me, pulling me down before I could get my legs underneath me.

"Please don't break an ankle."

Once down from the ledge, I was shoved right into the crowd of rioters. Police finally had the manpower and equipment to force everyone away from the complex.

Many rioters, deflated from being unable to get inside the Capitol, went in search of an easier target.

They found that target in the form of reporters and cameramen who were set up in the grassy area on the Capitol's east side. A mob started to surround them, with some erroneously claiming it was CNN. Some in the crowd started throwing objects at the reporters. The reporters scrambled to save as much of their equipment as they could but had to abandon most of it before being overrun.

To celebrate their "victory," the Capitol rioters used fists and flagpoles to smash cameras, tripods, monitors, sound equipment, and light stands.

They poured water all over anything that looked like it was powered by electricity. While filming the ordeal, I realized I had put myself in a bad spot when some of them noticed my giant "PRESS" patch on my ballistic vest. They started to point and shout at me. I frantically shouted back that I, too, hated fake news and was not with CNN. I decided not to press my luck and snuck a little bit away.

Once the mob was done with trashing the equipment, they went looking for other "fake news" outlets, but as far as I know, they didn't attack anyone else. Meanwhile, to add to the circus atmosphere, a man on an electric scooter was doing laps around the driveway of the Capitol, blaring the siren from *The Purge*.

By now it was getting close to the 6:00 p.m. curfew Washington Mayor Muriel Bowser had implemented. The number of law enforcement started to outnumber the crowd outside the complex. In addition to additional DC Metro Police officers, I saw a large contingent of FBI agents. The National Guard, in full riot gear, were now on the ground as well. In one large line, all the law enforcement agencies finally pushed everyone off of the Capitol grounds and into the street. The wave of protesters and rioters had finally receded. Trash was everywhere. I called it a night to head to the mobile studios to appear on Tucker Carlson's and Shannon Bream's shows to relay what I had experienced.

At the time of this writing, many months after January 6th, a lot of questions remain unanswered.

The first is why were the U.S. Capitol Police—responsible for securing the Capitol and its nearby office buildings—not fully prepared to handle such a large group of people that anyone could see were, at a minimum, going to try to enter the building? My theory is the Capitol Police leadership was complacent (as were their overseers in the Congressional leadership). The Capitol is the site of many protests throughout the year, so they must have thought to run the same playbook they always go by, which is to just have a meh number of officers, in non-riot gear, on the ground behind the easily moveable barricades.

What they did not account for was just how strongly those in attendance felt about the election. Moreover, they failed to consider how angry these people had been seeing Antifa, BLM, and their allies run riot—with impunity—throughout most of 2020. (Not that that justifies the riots of January 6th, but it should explain some motivations.)

The response from other law enforcement agencies and the National Guard was slow, but that was not necessarily their fault. A day before the riot, Mayor Bowser posted to Twitter the letter she sent to Acting Attorney General Jeffrey Rosen, Acting Secretary of Defense Christopher Miller, and Army Secretary Ryan McCarthy. In it she explained that she did not want extra federal law enforcement personnel in Washington on the day of the protest unless the city's police department was consulted first.

"The Metropolitan Police Department (MPD) is prepared for this week's First Amendment activities. MPD has coordinated with its federal partners, namely the US Park Police, US Capitol Police, and the US Secret Service—all of whom regularly have uniformed personnel protecting federal assets in the District of Columbia," Bowser wrote. She added, "The District of Columbia Government has not requested personnel from any other federal law enforcement agencies."

On top of that, Mayor Bowser only wanted 340 members of the DC National Guard activated, out of a force of around 1,100. And she wanted them unarmed and only helping conduct traffic.

According to NPR's timeline of the day's events, the city's request to activate more members of the DC National Guard was approved at

3:26 p.m., over an hour after the Capitol was breached. It was not until 5:02 p.m. that 154 additional members of the DC National Guard, now equipped for crowd control, departed the DC Armory towards the Capitol.[41]

In fairness, the District government does not have control over the Capitol's security. But by failing to have more National Guardsmen on hand, and refusing extra law enforcement help, it only served to increase the response time when events got out of hand.

Apparently, law enforcement agencies knew people would try to enter the Capitol, but, for whatever reason, the Capitol police were not prepared for what happened.

It is also worth asking if any law enforcement informants among the pro-Trump crowd were leading the charge during the early stages of the riot.

While it was good to see people condemn what happened, some on the Left, as usual, took things too far in their zeal.

Perhaps the most disgusting example of this is when a few Democrats or their allies in the media compared the Capitol riot to the 9/11 terrorist attacks in 2001. You know, the ones that killed almost 3,000 Americans.[42]

Republican-turned-Democratic consultant Matthew Dowd, for instance, told MSNBC's Joy Reid, "January 6th was worse than 9/11 because it's continued to rip our country apart."

Lincoln Project co-founder Steve Schmidt, meanwhile, said, "The 1/6 attack for the future of the country was a profoundly more dangerous event than the 9/11 attacks. And in the end, the 1/6 attacks are likely to kill a lot more Americans than were killed in the 9/11 attacks, which will include the casualties of the wars that lasted 20 years following."

The White House correspondent for Huffington Post, S.V. Dáte, tweeted, "Trump Apology Corps in full apology mode. The 9/11 terrorists and Osama bin Laden never threatened the heart of the American experiment. The 1/6 terrorists and Donald Trump absolutely did exactly that. Trump continues that effort today."

Another Twitter user countered, "United 93 was intended to crash into the Capitol. You think January 6th was worse than that?" to which Dáte replied, "1000 percent worse."

It should come as no surprise that 9/11 first responders took great offense to such comparisons.

One of them is my friend Rob O'Donnell. He was a detective with the New York City Police Department that day. He called his family to say a potential final goodbye before rushing to the Twin Towers. Over the following weeks, he spent countless hours combing through the rubble trying to locate survivors or, sadly, victims' remains. Hearing people compare the Capitol riot to 9/11 infuriated O'Donnell.

"This comparison in theory may sound hip or symbolic," he told me. "In reality, it's like comparing getting hit in the face with an aluminum baseball bat by Barry Bonds (9/11) versus getting poked with an index finger by one of the Olsen Twins (January 6th). That is how ludicrous this comparison is to those who lived 9/11."

He added, "I was literally walking through the visible remnants of thousands of Americans for months starting on 9/11. A few bumps and bruises, busted egos, minor vandalism, and misdemeanor trespassing, along with a handful of exacerbated natural cause deaths, however tragic, don't fit into the same conversation."

O'Donnell noted if people want to compare the government's incompetence to preventing both incidents, "there may be more common ground." He noted that agency tribalism and failure to share information, or to act on warnings and follow up on actionable intelligence helped lead to 9/11.

"On January 6th, we had local leaders failing to accept help and resources because of political tribalism. [They] failed to support local agencies and prepare due to anti-police rhetoric."

Among the other frustrating aspects from the fallout of the Capitol riot was how many within the BLM movement, the mainstream media, and Democratic political circles tried to rewrite the history of the summer riots to criticize how police handled the breach at the Capitol.

The day after the January 6th riots, Vice President-elect Kamala Harris said, "We witnessed two systems of justice when we saw one that let extremists storm the United States Capitol, and another that released tear gas on peaceful protesters last summer...We know this is unacceptable.

We know we should be better than this."[43]

The narrative held that if this had been a crowd of black and brown people, the police would have been slaughtering them, but they were more than okay with letting white people inside the building. After all, this line of thinking goes, police all across the country had behaved brutally against "peaceful" BLM protesters during the summer of 2020.

George Orwell could hardly have come up with a better example of Doublespeak.

You've probably seen some variation of a meme depicting National Guardsmen protecting the Lincoln Memorial during the BLM riots and complaining this was the government's response to the "mostly peaceful protests."

The irony—and something this meme sorely fails to appreciate—is that not only did officials largely fail to protect America's cities during the 2020 riots, they failed to protect our monuments as well. Many of the monuments on the National Mall were vandalized during summer 2020, most notably the World War II Memorial and Lincoln Memorial.[44]

The National Guard *was* called in to protect those memorials, but only after the fact. They were deployed on the Mall in order to prevent *further* destruction. Countless smaller monuments, memorials, and statues across the country received no such protections.

Yet despite the riots the nation's capital experienced, Speaker of the House Nancy Pelosi denounced the troops on the steps of the Lincoln Memorial as an "alarming" step to take in order to protect federal property.[45]

This narrative could not be further from the truth.

From the very beginning, the Capitol Police, and eventually the other federal and local law enforcement agencies, did everything in their power to prevent rioters from entering the complex. They used pepper balls, pepper spray, tear gas, flashbangs, and rubber bullets to repel rioters.

(There is one video that shows officers letting a crowd enter through one doorway, which certainly raises concerns, but that appears to be a lone exception. In virtually every other case—and there are miles of video documenting this—police tried to hold the line on January 6th.)

The attempt to rewrite history adds insult to literal injuries. Some police officers were dragged from their defensive lines and almost beaten by the rioters. At least one officer was caught on video being crushed, with blood coming out of his mouth and begging for help, after being trapped between the crowd and a door.

The Left's false narrative about January 6th also ignores the reason that riots of any kind were able to occur across America during 2020. Local police were often outnumbered, or they did not want to do serious policing out of fear of adding fuel to the anger that was exploding, or they were ordered by superiors to stand down.

You need look no further than when the Minneapolis police were forced to abandon the 3rd Precinct. Or when Seattle Mayor Jenny Durkan ordered the SPD to abandon their East Precinct in an attempt to appease the BLM mob that was rioting right outside day after day. That move not only failed to placate the crowd, it allowed CHAZers to hold an entire neighborhood hostage for almost a month.

The Left's false narrative also ignores the fact someone *was* shot by Capitol police. Ashli Babbitt, a white, 14-year Air Force veteran, was shot and killed after trying to enter the Speaker's lobby through a broken window. Regardless of whether or not the shooting was justified (the officer was neither charged nor disciplined), the color of the victim exposes the lie at the heart of the Left's argument.

Another narrative I have to address—this one pushed by some on the Right—is that Antifa and BLM "infiltrators" were mainly responsible for the violence on January 6th.

This mirrors the argument many liberals made in 2020 to blame "right-wing infiltrators" for the BLM riots. Putting aside the fact many of those who broke into the Capitol have been identified and their support for Trump and far-right conspiracy theories were revealed, the main reason that I *know* the majority of those who went into the Capitol were not Antifa activists is because so few did not try to hide their identities.

Quite a few individuals who have been charged for their involvement on January 6th bragged about their involvement on social media—that's how so many were identified in the first place.

Antifa groups, on the other hand, go to great lengths to prevent media from filming their exploits. And they take extreme measures to keep from being identified, often wearing masks, kerchiefs, or balaclavas while in the streets. My guess is that many of those who entered the Capitol were surprised they got as far as they did.

It is worth noting the case of BLM activist John Sullivan, who was among the first to breach the Capitol and recorded himself egging on the people he was with.

In the end, the Capitol rioters gave Democrats and the mainstream media the mother of all hall passes to seek out and destroy their political opponents whether they were at the Capitol or not.

To be clear, I am against rioting in every case. Rioting is often built off of a faulty premise. It harms innocent people who had nothing to do with whatever is said to have sparked it in the first place.

What happened at the Capitol was no exception. The hypocrisy from Democrats and the mainstream media was disgusting to see. They had minimized, were slow to condemn, or even cheered on the orgies of violence of 2020. Gone were the days when "All Cops Are Bastards" and "It's just a building, there's insurance." At least they had caught up to the rest of us who were against riots from the start. If only they were sincere and not just trying to score political points.

Perhaps one of the weirdest outcomes of the Capitol riot came after a swimming news outlet, SwimSwam, reached out to me to ask if the video I took in the Rotunda was all I had. By the time I replied, they had already published the story that was the reason for the inquiry: They were the first to report that Olympic gold medalist swimmer Klete Keller was among those inside the Rotunda.

I had no idea who Keller was, but for anyone plugged into the world of swimming, he was easy to spot in my video for two reasons: He stands 6'6", and he wore his Olympic swimming jacket at the Capitol.[46]

In my video, Keller does not appear to be among those who were actively fighting the cops. But he was present inside the Capitol.

Was January 6th an "insurrection," as so many have called it? I believe that term gives the mob more credit than it deserves. Many of those who made it into the Capitol—Klete Keller being a perfect example—had no clue what to do once they got inside. Some people acted like tourists taking in the sights—snapping photos in the Rotunda or possibly grabbing a souvenir.

More than once people approached me in the Capitol to ask what the "plan" was, to which I responded with a variation of, "I have no idea. I just followed you guys in here."

That's why I use the term "riot" to describe what happened at the Capitol. Similar to the 2020 riots, January 6th was a chaotic, mob-mentality-driven event with no clear leader or plan.

There are those who want to call what happened on January 6 an insurrection, mostly Democrats and the media. But their credibility is shot because they refuse to apply the term to similar actions taken during the civil unrest in 2020.

This was exemplified during Rep. Adam Kinzinger's (R-IL) opening remarks on the House select committee investigating the Capitol riot. He said the reason Congress needed to investigate what happened is because "there is a difference between breaking the law and rejecting the rule of law, between a crime, even grave crimes, and a coup."

Let's take his talking point and the definition of insurrection, which is "an act or instance of revolting against civil authority or an established government."

With that in mind, look at what happened at the 3rd Precinct in Minneapolis on May 28. Protesters and rioters focused much of their attention and anger towards the 3rd Precinct, where Derek Chauvin had been assigned.

Sure, there was plenty of looting at nearby stores, but rioters tried for almost a week to take over the police building. The mob eventually succeeded once the mayor ordered the police to abandon their post. Even as the police were fleeing, they continued to be attacked by the mob. When the officers were gone, the rioters ransacked the precinct, eventually setting it on fire. Quite a rejection of the "rule of law" and a revolt "against civil authority," if you ask me.

How about the month-long siege at the Mark O. Hatfield Courthouse in Portland, Oregon, which is federal property? Multiple officers were injured during the nightly attacks. An actual bomb, not a large firework, was thrown at the building.

This seems to fit any definition of an "insurrection." Yet it was downplayed, excused, or ignored by many of those people who, after January 6th, professed grave concern about riots.

If you spent 2020 downplaying or trying to excuse the widespread destruction that took place across the country, with everyday Americans bearing the brunt when law and order vanished, I don't particularly care what you have to say about the Capitol riot.

CAPITOL AFTERMATH

I was originally booked to appear on Shannon Bream's show *before* the riots occurred. When the events of the day exploded, Tucker Carlson's people were able to work it out to where I could appear on his show the same day as well, which is something guests are not typically allowed to do. No commercial breaks either. I made my way to the Sheraton Pentagon City Hotel where I was to meet up with the mobile studio truck since the normal studio in D.C. was completely booked with guests.

At the hotel, I ran into Richie McGinniss and Drew Hernandez, who were also slated to be interviewed on FOX News. We were still in shock from what we had been through.

I discovered that Richie and I had been right next to each other in the Rotunda, but hadn't noticed each other (gas masks will do that). Richie ended up filming one of the more comic scenes of the day: a man wearing American flag pants casually firing up a joint under the Capitol dome.

Later that evening I sneezed and coughed as I started to remove my ballistic vest and jacket. The CS powder still heavily coated my clothes, and the pepper spray that had hit my exposed skin was starting to burn again after I washed my hands and splashed water on my face.

The pain brought to mind the danger I'd experienced that afternoon, when the pressing and panicking crowds in the Capitol corridor led me, however briefly, to consider the possibility I would be crushed there.

I called a friend of mine, still trying to process what happened. "I thought I was going to suffocate in the Rotunda," I told him. "Which, considering where else I've come close to biting it, isn't such a terrible place, I guess."

It was past midnight when I finally arrived home after an incredibly long and draining day. Instead of going straight to bed, however, I pulled out the "final will and testament" documentation the Marine Corps gave us when my Reserve unit was preparing to be activated for COVID-19 response during the early days of the pandemic.

I was to be attached to the Personnel Retrieval and Processing Company, commonly known as the body baggers. If we ended up being activated, I was going to help process the high volume of coronavirus remains.

The activation order never came, but the will was nice to have if the worst-case scenario ever happened during the riots.

I kept it on my desk during the summer of 2020 so it would be easy for my roommates, Logan and Greg, to find if necessary.

I put the will away after Joe Biden was declared the winner of the 2020 election. I became complacent. The riots were basically over, I thought.

How wrong I was.

Needless to say, the document will be on my desk for the foreseeable future.

7

"Mostly True" Media Coverage

I HAVE largely worked in conservative media throughout my career. Conservative media exists because people see through the false pretenses of the supposedly "objective" mainstream media. They hunger for truly objective reporting on what's going on, whether about government and politics, the economy, or the culture at large. People recognize there are large holes in what the mainstream media regularly provides, gaps and distortions about the news that are caused by politically driven journalism from people who claim to be apolitical in their work.

Conservative media emerged to fill the breach, which might seem ironic given the word "conservative" in the name. But the truth is that conservative media outlets that openly profess their ideological inclinations are typically far more objective, and committed to straightforward reporting than the supposedly objective mainstream press.

Conservative media outlets are iconoclastic and contrarian. They gladly examine and even burst the liberal pieties that polite society (i.e., the Mandarins in the mainstream media and Washington's permanent political establishment) has accepted for years without question. Conservative media is alternative media in the very best sense of the term, which helps explain the success of FOX News that so enrages the Left.

During my time working in the D.C. Bubble, I've seen the media constantly mislead for political purposes, particularly when reporting on President Trump and his administration.

The riots of 2020 were hardly different. Much of the reporting and commentary about them read as if it had been written by the Ministry of Propaganda—promoting a party line whether the facts supported it or not.

The seeds for the misleading coverage of America's urban unrest that dominated the summer of 2020 were sown the previous January. I saw it firsthand.

On January 20, I traveled to Richmond, Virginia, to cover the Virginia Citizens Defense League's annual Lobby Day. The VCDL is a prominent gun-rights group, something of a National Rifle Association on steroids but confined to one state.

The 2020 gathering promised to be significant because Virginia Democrats, led by Gov. Ralph Northam and supported by majorities in both houses of the state legislature, planned to move on several extreme gun control bills in the coming legislative session. The 2020 Lobby Day would presage the fight to come.

Before the gathering even took place, liberals in the mainstream media began slandering VCDL's Lobby Day as a "white nationalist" gathering. Some claimed it had the potential to be the next Charlottesville-level event because many attendees planned on openly carrying rifles, shotguns, and handguns.

The day before the event, NBC reporter Ben Collins, the outlet's go-to for online extremism, tweeted: "Reporters covering tomorrow's white nationalist rally in Virginia, I'm absolutely begging you: Verify information before you send it out tomorrow, even if it's a very sensational rumor you heard from a cop." He added, "Don't become a hero in neo-Nazi propaganda circles with made-up stuff." (He would later delete the tweet.)

Collins defended his claim because, in the days leading up to the event, six suspected Neo-Nazis were arrested for allegedly planning some sort of violence at the rally.[47]

Not to be outdone, Talia Lavin, a freelance writer often published in many liberal outlets, tweeted, "The event in Richmond tomorrow is a white nationalist rally because if you knowingly make common cause with nazis you're a fuckin' nazi."

She added, "if I were not a nazi I would simply not attend an event that I knew would be swarming with nazis."[48] (Keep in mind this is the same Talia Lavin who lost her job as a *New Yorker* fact-checker because she had accused a wounded U.S. Marine combat veteran who worked for US Immigration Enforcement and Customs of having a Nazi tattoo. It was actually a tattoo of his unit's logo.[49])

The neo-Nazi angle was irresistible for journalists themselves disposed to the sort of gun-control efforts Democrats were offering. It allowed them to condemn the entire event as a racist gathering, a guilt-by-association narrative too good to pass up.

A segment by MSNBC anchor Craig Melvin describing the rally read, "Thousands of gun rights activists, white nationalists, militia groups all swarming the state capitol in Richmond." It was a perfect narrative for the Left.

Never mind that the group's president, Philip Van Cleave, forcefully denounced racism during the event. It almost seemed liberals and the media were wishing for a shooting of some kind to happen to help prove their anti-gun point.

This was Virginia, so perhaps it was no surprise to see a handful of Confederate flags. Of course, these were vastly outnumbered by the American flags other protesters were carrying. There were also hundreds of minorities in attendance, many armed. To call it a "Nazi" or "white nationalist" rally was simply not true.

As a Latino, I felt perfectly safe—perhaps the safest and most peaceful protest of all the ones I covered in 2020. (My only complaint was the cold weather.) There was no looting, no burning of buildings. To my knowledge, nobody fired their weapon. Lines were orderly. People were courteous and friendly to all, regardless of race.

Thousands of people gathered peacefully to exercise their First and Second Amendment rights. Naturally, the media ignored that, so desperate were they to claim otherwise.

Fast forward five months to Seattle, where the media used the same playbook to distort the public's understanding of what was happening in CHAZ.

"If you've been getting your news from right-wing media, you probably think armed militant Antifa activists have seized a section of Seattle," tweeted CNN Senior Media Reporter Oliver Darcy. "But the mayor's office tells me, 'City officials have not interacted with 'armed antifa militants' at this site.'"[50]

In the story accompanying his tweet, Darcy admitted Antifa is a group that exists. However, he leaned on the clearly disingenuous claims of city officials to debunk the "right-wing media's" narrative. Anyone who was on the ground in Seattle—I was one of them—could see that "armed militant Antifa activists" had indeed seized a section of Seattle. Whether or not city officials had interacted with them (spoiler alert: they had, despite their claims) didn't change the fact that armed individuals dressed in the black garb of Antifa were prominently positioned among those calling shots in CHAZ.

Efforts to prevent the darker side of CHAZ/CHOP from being reported were a staple of everyday life in the zone. On multiple occasions my attempts to record fistfights or scuffles between occupiers were thwarted by residents preventing me from filming. Media censorship was the rule in CHAZ/CHOP; only the "good" news could be reported. That's something that CNN and other mainstream outlets never mentioned to their viewers and readers, though they all knew it was happening.

Which leads us to the "FIERY BUT MOSTLY PEACEFUL" scenes in Kenosha, as CNN would infamously describe the situation. When I saw the notorious chyron running beneath CNN reporter Omar Jimenez's report, I laughed. I assumed it was a photoshopped screenshot, and a very well done one at that.

"There's no way they would do something like that after MSNBC's BS in Minneapolis."

But lo and behold, it *was* real.

Frankly, that incident performed a valuable service. It exposed in the clearest terms that what the mainstream media says is happening, and what *actually* is happening, are often two very different things.

CNN's overt denial of reality—a reality its viewers could see with their own eyes—was as if a Weather Channel reporter checking in from the middle of a hurricane, wind howling and water up to his knees, insisted it was just a mostly cloudy day.

It was enough to make one wonder if former Iraqi Information Minister Mohammed Saeed al-Sahhaf—aka Baghdad Bob—was moonlighting as a producer at CNN.

The deliberate misframing of the riots was not reserved solely for television. Prestigious print publications got in on the act as well. *The Washington Post's* official Twitter account, for instance, tweeted an article about the Jacob Blake shooting with the caption, "Police use tear gas on hundreds protesting shooting in Kenosha, Wis."[51]

How odd, since the article's actual copy gave a fuller—and different—account than the snippet provided in the tweet: "In Kenosha, those have included burned buildings, ransacked stores and nights of apparent lawlessness as rioters have inflicted damage with few signs of a police presence. Some who gathered in the city threw firecrackers, toppled streetlights, smashed storefronts and set fires, while police launched tear gas and fired beanbag-like projectiles."

Reading the tweet, one would have thought it was a modern-day version of Bull Connor turning the firehoses on civil rights marchers, rather than police combatting rampaging looters and rioters whose actions threatened to kill innocent people and destroy entire city blocks.

The misinformation propagated by the mainstream media regarding Kenosha was not just limited to the riots. Coverage of the Jacob Blake and Kyle Rittenhouse cases gave ample opportunity for the mainstream media to step on rake after rake.

In Blake's case, the most egregious error was the media's claim that he was not armed when he was shot. One has to assume that considerably added to the rage that spilled out into the streets of Kenosha.

The claim was utterly false, yet it was repeated incessantly:

- "People in Kenosha County, Wisconsin, have been ordered to stay inside under a curfew starting at 8 p.m. CT tonight following the police shooting of unarmed Black man Jacob Blake"—*CNN Breaking News*[52]
- "Athletes spoke out after footage surfaced of Jacob Blake, an unarmed Black man, being shot by police"—ESPN[53]
- "And this morning there's still no explanation for why police in Kenosha, Wisconsin, shot an unarmed black man in the back multiple times. This is not the first time that the police there have done something like [that]."—*CNN anchor Alisyn Camerota*
- "We are following a disturbing story out of Kenosha, Wisconsin, where police shot an unarmed black man right in front of his children"—*CNN anchor Wolf Blitzer*
- "More protests erupt overnight in Kenosha, Wisconsin, where police shot an unarmed black man seven times in the back in front of his children"—*CNN anchor Anderson Cooper, while a chyron scrolling below read, "MORE PROTESTS ERUPT OVER POLICE SHOOTING OF UNARMED BLACK MAN"*
- "Continuing protests overnight in Wisconsin amidst these grizzly new details about controversial police shooting. Wisconsin police

repeatedly firing at an unarmed black man as he walked away
from them and into a car where his children were inside"
—*MSNBC anchor Ari Melber*

- "'They shot my son se...seven time...seven times, like he didn't
  matter. But my son matters': Jacob Blake Sr., the father of the
  unarmed Black man shot by police spoke at a conference at the
  Kenosha County Courthouse"—*Reuters*[54]

- "Joe Biden responds to the shooting of Jacob Blake, the unarmed
  Black man shot in the back by a police officer in Kenosha, Wis.,
  over the weekend"—*POLITICO, August 26th*[55]

The lie undoubtedly was repeated so often not because so many journalists wished to traffic in falsehood (though some do) but because, well,
the point about Blake being unarmed was mentioned everywhere. Everyone knew it. It had to be true, right?

What a flimsy basis on which to make bold claims and fundamental
assertions. At least it's a slightly understandable explanation.

But how to explain the completely willful telling of a lie?

That scenario presented itself in January 2021 when Kenosha County
District Attorney Michael Graveley explained why he was not charging
the officers involved in the shooting. Part of the reason for his decision,
he said, was because Blake had been armed with a knife and threatened
officers.

A pretty straightforward explanation. But you'd be mistaken if you
were counting on the media to cover it fairly.

Shortly after Gravely's announcement, *The Washington Post* tweeted,
"Blake, who witnesses said had been trying to break up an argument
between two women, was unarmed and shot as he walked back toward
his vehicle." After being hounded by social media users (and likely after consultation with the *Post*'s attorneys), the paper quietly deleted the
tweet and issued a correction.[56]

Another common narrative pushed along by the mainstream media
was that Kyle Rittenhouse shot three people in Kenosha during a *protest*.

Simply not true. There were indeed peaceful protests that occurred
during the day. But that's not when the Rittenhouse shootings took
place. It was after it turned dark, and *rioters* had taken over the streets

causing mayhem and violence, that the fateful events involving Ritten-house occurred (documented in Chapter 4).

That was hardly the only media misstep with regard to the Rittenhouse case. Journalists routinely mangled key facts about the case, from report-ing on the internal DHS background memo about the shootings to ele-ments of the November 2021 trial in which Rittenhouse was acquitted on all counts. Whether errors were intentional or merely the result of sloppy newsgathering, they don't reflect well on the media.

Similar to the Kenosha narrative, some in the media tried to paint the Louisville riots as "mostly peaceful." Those occurred after a grand jury refused to indict police officers involved in Breonna Taylor's fatal shooting on murder charges.

I was on ground in Louisville that night. The situation quickly deterio-rated after the grand jury's decision was announced. It was *anything* but peaceful.

I witnessed members of a large group of protesters in Jefferson Square Park facing off with local police.

"All y'all get ready to fucking die!" one man screamed at officers.

A U-Haul truck parked along the route was filled with premade shields and banners for the marchers to use.

"Shields! There's shields in the truck!" one woman screamed, sparking a mad dash from the crowd to grab everything out of the truck.

As the crowd moved further away from the downtown area and into the city's neighborhoods, some in the mob began to damage restaurants' outdoor seating areas.[57]

I was on the sidewalk at the very edge of the crowd. A shoving match broke out nearby between agitators and the police. I cannot say for sure who started it, but that's when police started to move in, using batons and pepper balls to disperse the crowd. While many in the crowd ran away, some remained to fight with officers.

I almost got caught in the fighting. I and other members of the media were complying with the officers' orders to leave when one man near us shouted to not move back. He grabbed firmly onto an iron fence with his left hand and spread out his right arm in an attempt to physically stop us from moving backwards.

This was problematic since the police were still moving forward. I shoved the man's right arm away from me, and I got around him. After more shoving from other media members, he gave up. Since I wanted to document the ongoing fighting and arrests, I swung open the iron fence's gate and closed it behind me.

After things settled down, I tried to leave through the front gate, but the officers wouldn't let me, so I went out the back of the property where we were, admittedly, trespassing.

Most of the members of that confrontational crowd had been arrested or dispersed, but the day was far from over. With my friend and colleague Shelby Talcott, I walked three miles back to Jefferson Square Park where people were again gathering. On our trek, we saw more than 20 police cars speeding back downtown. We took off running to try to get back as soon as possible. As day turned to evening, the crowd grew more unruly.

The situation soon spiraled out of control. Multiple fires were started in different areas of the park. Large garbage piles were set aflame, with one exploding right in front of me (I suspect an aerosol can cooked off).

Rioters tried to set the Hall of Justice ablaze, with others shielding their attempts with umbrellas to block the view and with shouts and threats directed at the press to not film what was happening.

"Burn it down!" the crowd shouted.

Officers inside the Hall of Justice rushed out with riot shields to repel the arsonists and put out the fires. While using fire extinguishers to douse the flames, rioters pelted them with rocks and other projectiles.

Officers posted on the roofs of nearby buildings informed the rioters over loudspeakers that the gathering had been declared an unlawful assembly. If they did not leave the area, they would be subjected to crowd control munitions. Fair warning.

Most rioters did leave, smashing windows of surrounding buildings, damaging bus stops, and setting more fires during their retreat.

Though many fled in different directions, one group of rioters started marching directly toward a line of police officers blocking the road.

The officers on the rooftops started firing flashbangs. That was not unexpected, particularly given the warning offered moments before.

What *was* unexpected was the loud ringing of gunshots just off to our left. That really got people scattering.

I grabbed Shelby and ran one way, but police vehicles starting to move in blocked our exit. We veered in the opposite direction, barely making it across the street before a van full of police officers stopped to help set up the perimeter. Walking away, safe for the moment, I received a text informing me that a police officer had been shot. Then I saw another officer had been shot.

"Good thing I have rifle plates now."

Shelby and I headed for the hospital where the two wounded officers were being treated. Local police and Kentucky National Guard were protecting the hospital to prevent anyone from even thinking about attacking the building. Fortunately, we soon learned, the two officers were expected to recover from their injuries.

Any reasonable reader of this account would see this was *not* a "mostly peaceful" or even partly peaceful protest. But the facts hardly stopped the unreasonable editors at Reuters from pushing that false narrative.

"Demonstrations in Louisville wore on past nightfall in defiance of a 9 p.m. curfew and remained mostly peaceful until several gunshots rang out in the midst of a skirmish between protesters and heavily armed police." That's what Reuters tweeted *after* officers were shot and after wanton acts of destruction had been committed.[58]

Reporters at different news outlets routinely took it upon themselves to try to dismiss people's concerns that their neighborhood could be the next place where riots would occur.

"Dropping a piece shortly with [Ben Collins]. Turns out antifa wasn't coming to your suburbs, but Qanon is about to roll through," NBC News reporter Brandy Zadrozny wrote in a since deleted tweet.[59] (Yes, that's the same Ben Collins from earlier.)

The story they wrote delved into the #SavetheChildren rallies protesting child sex trafficking, events that had ties to the Qanon conspiracy theorists. The story itself was perfectly legitimate. However, the timing was terrible. The authors' flippant dismissal of Antifa and BLM rioting in neighborhoods was tweeted out just two days before Kenosha went up in flames. Ouch.

NBC News hardly had the monopoly on snotty and condescending commentary.

CNN correspondent Josh Campbell tweeted, "Good morning from wonderful Portland, where the city is not under siege and buildings are not burning to the ground. I also ate my breakfast burrito outside today and so far haven't been attacked by shadowy gangs of Antifa commandos."[60]

CNN "Reliable Sources" host Brian Stelter wrote in his newsletter regarding the riots outside the federal courthouse: "Right-wing media ramped up its coverage of scattered unrest in Portland, Oregon.... Evidently a small group of self-described anarchists suddenly deserved national news coverage."[61]

Stelter's and Campbell's CNN colleague Chris Cilliza wrote on CNN. com that "Trump's efforts to label what is happening in major cities as 'riots' speaks at least somewhat to his desperation, politically speaking, at the moment."[62]

In a move that can only be described as either pure master trolling or complete lack of situational awareness, the featured image accompanying Cilliza's piece was of B&L Office Furniture completely engulfed in flames during the Kenosha riots.

The sort of mindset behind such asinine comments and observations was on full display in September 2020, when the Associated Press announced they were sanitizing riot coverage for the latest edition of its *AP Stylebook*.

AP explained, "Focusing on rioting and property destruction rather than underlying grievance has been used in the past to stigmatize broad swaths of people protesting against lynching, police brutality or for racial justice, going back to the urban uprisings of the 1960s."

Never mind the riots had been occurring for a large portion of the year throughout the country, including in suburban areas. The more the riots continued, the more apparent it became that so many reporters' narratives were aging poorly.

An unusual development began to emerge in late summer in American cities experiencing unrest. Protesters were becoming much more confrontational. *The New York Times* detailed how BLM-aligned protesters would march through the residential areas of Portland, Oregon, targeting residents who did not express fervent support for the movement. This included harassing a black man who defended his neighbor from agitators upset he was flying an American flag.[63]

Residential areas of Washington, DC, meanwhile saw anti-police agitators harassing people trying to eat at restaurants' outdoor dining areas. Diners were coerced to throw up their fists to show solidarity. If they refused, they were surrounded and shouted at. Some residents were also harassed at their homes for not showing solidarity.

One married couple, we'll call them Samantha and Patrick, were accosted three separate times during the "Fuck the Police" marches that occurred in the DuPont Circle neighborhood. In one instance, they filmed the crowd throwing fireworks into their small yard, scaring the couple's dog. When they went outside to tell them to stop, they were met with cries of "Fuck you" and even more fireworks being thrown at them.

"They also graffitied our building, the sidewalk, and cars with violent messages," the couple told me. "When they began to leave, they shouted they knew 'where you live' and that 'we'll be back.' In all sincerity, I am afraid of what could happen the next time they come around."

That same month, a pro-BLM crowd attacked diners eating outside in Rochester, New York. The mob threw objects, broke glassware, and overturned tables and chairs, forcing patrons to flee to safety.

"We're shutting your party down!" a woman can be heard screaming on a video taken of the assault.[64]

The most damning piece of evidence refuting reporters' casual dismissals of the 2020 riots came when I was on the ground in a Milwaukee suburb in October.

The Milwaukee District Attorney decided to not charge Wauwatosa, Wisconsin, police officer Joseph Mensah for the shooting death of 17-year-old Alvin Cole, a black teenager. Like much of America, I had been unaware of the incident when it occurred in February, before COVID-19 and before the George Floyd incident.

The DA's decision not to charge appears perfectly reasonable. Officer Mensah, who himself is black, fatally shot Cole after Cole refused to drop the handgun he was carrying. Cole had already fired his gun, and was pointing it in the direction of Mensah and his fellow officers. Mensah fired five times, killing Cole.

The incident may have occurred pre-George Floyd, but the DA's decision not to charge came in a post-George Floyd world. It did not matter what the reasoning was, or what the facts of the case might be. A black man had been shot and killed by police. Riots were bound to happen. Public outrage was heightened partly due to Mensah having killed two other people in the line of duty previously.[65]

Shortly after the announcement, a crowd of protesters started out in nearby Milwaukee but then began to caravan towards Wauwatosa. It was dark by the time I arrived at the scene in full gear.

I got near the protesters right as they started to enter Wauwatosa's city limits. Once in the area, some began smashing storefront windows. A Kumon learning center owned by a Lebanese immigrant was damaged, along with a dry cleaners that was owned by Asian immigrants. No one in the caravan of protesters tried to stop the rioters from their destructive acts.

As the crowd moved on, though, something else caught my eye. People were dashing from the street towards a small housing complex nearby. I then saw, and recorded, rioters throwing rocks at the residential building. Glass can be heard shattering, and the window blinds could be seen moving inward with each rock thrown.

Credit must be given where some is due: Others in the caravan stepped in to stop these rioters—"That's somebody's home!"—but by then, the damage was already done. And a dangerous line had been crossed.

The rioting hardly stopped there. The caravan waged battle with the police, hurling projectiles at officers and, in turn, trying to dodge pepper balls and tear gas canisters. Some began looting a Speedway gas station.

The mayhem and violence continued as the caravan progressed deeper and deeper into Wauwatosa neighborhoods. Drivers of cars that found themselves caught in the melee made desperate U-turns in people's yards to escape.

The next morning, I went back to the areas that had been hit. I was caught off guard. The now-quiet streets, complete with homes decorated for fall, looked almost exactly like my suburban hometown of Wheaton, Illinois. The riots in Wauwatosa the night before drove home to me that no city or town was safe from a marauding crowd emboldened by a flimsy excuse.

I found the owner of the apartment complex that had been attacked cleaning the mess rioters had left. He told me that one person, a 70-year-old woman, had been home when the apartment building was attacked.

"She was in her bedroom, and her front window got smashed," he told me. "She screamed; she started crying. She called me, by the time I got here…she couldn't stop shaking. I ended up loading her up into my vehicle and driving her to her sister's house in Grafton in hopes she would get some rest because I knew she wouldn't get rest here overnight."

Other tenants, he said, had left town the day before out of concern for their safety.

He said the rioters caused around $100,000 in damage in just a few short moments of destruction before being stopped by other protesters.

"I understand the right to protest," he said. "I'm completely behind that. But when you damage somebody's residence, you've gone too far; it's not a protest anymore."

As the caravan had moved through different neighborhoods the evening before, they lingered in one area and, specifically, near the home of a white resident named Jason Fritz. I witnessed Fritz come outside to tell the crowd to move off his lawn, which included people riding dirt bikes and doing burnouts on his grass. He pleaded with the protesters to be mindful of where they were. According to Fritz, a lot of teachers and union members live in the area, potential allies of theirs.

When I interviewed him the next day, he told me how the protesters mocked him for owning his own house, yet have "no idea the struggle I went through to get this house. How I haven't had a vacation in 14 years so I could save up after my wife [had] a bankruptcy, adopting a child with special needs."

He elaborated: "I work really hard for these things, and that's what really upsets me. [My family] went through a lot of financially difficult times, from the time we got engaged all the way to now. We have gone through such trials and tribulations…I know how hard we work to put food on the table, to send our kids to the kind of private school to get them the kind of education we want."

He described the toll that COVID had placed on his family in the months leading up to the confrontation with protesters. "I'm not comfortable. I've been sitting at home since March, with my business destroyed, with my finances really harmed, with my kids trying to homeschool them."

Fritz explained his home was the last shred of dignity he had to be able to provide for his family during these difficult times. Seeing people desecrate it and mock him, solely because he is white while knowing nothing of his circumstances really hurt him.[66]

I could go on and on with examples of how people's fears of riots moving away from city centers and into residential neighborhoods were realized. Needless to say, however, there was little follow-up from Brandy Zadrozny, Brian Collins, Brian Stelter, or any of the other media mavens who had previously dismissed the idea of 2020's urban violence migrating to terrorize Americans in their homes.

"No matter the city, the liberal media will always give aid and comfort to the radical leftists looking to cause emotional and physical harm to otherwise peaceful citizens and their livelihoods," Curtis Houck told me.

Houck is managing editor of the Media Research Center's News-Busters media watchdog website. "If we had a serious news media in this country, there would be a lot more attention paid to the loss of property that's more than just buildings or stores but rather the representation of someone's life being ransacked."

CNN's Chris Cuomo essentially proved Houck's point about the media's lack of seriousness on this score. Cuomo raised eyebrows on his program by actually coming to the defense of destructive and violent protests.

"Please, show me where it says that protests are supposed to be polite and peaceful," Cuomo said during his June 2 program. "Because I can show you that outraged citizens are what made the country what she is and led to any major milestone. To be honest, this is not a tranquil time." He added, "Too many see the protests as the problem. No, the problem is what forced your fellow citizens to take the streets: persistent and poisonous inequities and injustice."[67]

A very disturbing and aggravating trend among many in the mainstream media was a shift from "Mostly peaceful protests" to "Riots? What riots?" that largely occurred in early 2021.

New York Times columnist Paul Krugman, for instance, tweeted in April, "Given that GOP supporters believe that rampaging mobs burned and looted major cities—somehow without the people actually living in those cities noticing—getting them to see facts about something as abstract as the deficit is a hopeless cause."[68] Keep in mind this comment came after an entire year of unrest from coast to coast.

Around the same time, *Washington Post* columnist Paul Waldman tweeted, "Important to understand that conservatives have been told, and they believe, that last summer many of America's cities were LITERALLY BURNED TO THE GROUND by BLM protesters. I am not exaggerating."[69]

Other examples were more subtle, like in a *New York Times* story from reporter Jennifer Medina about Latinos voting for Republicans: "Some of the frustrations voiced by Hispanic Republican men are stoked by misinformation, including conspiracy theories claiming that the 'deep state' took over during the Trump administration, and a belief that Black Lives Matter protests caused widespread violence."[70]

On January 17th, 2021, the *Times* published an article by reporter Astead Herndon in which he wrote, "For months, Republicans have used last summer's protests as a political catchall, highlighting isolated instances of property destruction and calls to defund the police to motivate their base in November."[71]

Ironically, Herndon's story was describing ways Republicans were downplaying the Capitol riot, only for him to downplay the massive destruction that occurred across the country caused by BLM and BLM-adjacent rioters.

Consider, too, a May *New York Times* op-ed from deputy opinion editor Patrick Healy. He accused respondents in a focus group who were influenced by FOX News and other conservative programming of "overstating the scattered street violence last summer."[72]

Telling people that riots were merely peaceful protests with a little bit of unrest, or even flat-out denying that they occurred is gaslighting. Pure and simple. It was crystal clear that the riots were a serious problem the country was experiencing.

I know. I was there, in city after city. I witnessed the destruction first-hand and chronicled its effects on people. I saw buildings torched. I saw innocent people beaten and attacked. I saw livelihoods destroyed. I saw lives broken.

I was there. What I didn't see were Paul Krugman or other "journalists" and commentators who couldn't be bothered to leave their makeshift home studios and offices to accurately report on what was happening, yet said it was not as big a deal as "conservative media" was making it out to be.

No wonder so many Americans view the mainstream media as out-of-touch city dwellers whose only purpose is to parrot liberal narratives, facts be damned.

I was there, along with other members of the Riot Squad. And because we presented facts that ran counter to the orthodox media narrative about the BLM riots, it was only a matter of time before we found ourselves in the crosshairs of the progressive media.

I was traveling in Texas when I noticed someone tagged me on Twitter in a comment that did not make a whole lot of sense. That's not an unusual occurrence. What *was* unusual, I noticed, was that the account being responded to was *The Intercept*, the muckraking lefty website that first gained prominence for reporting on the national security secrets disclosed by Edward Snowden.

The Intercept had tweeted the first two minutes of a video with the caption, "MEET THE RIOT SQUAD: RIGHT-WING REPORTERS WHOSE VIRAL VIDEOS ARE USED TO SMEAR BLM." The video and accompanying article came courtesy of *The Intercept*'s Robert Mackey and Travis Mannon.[73]

Now, I can only speak to my work; I'll let the others speak for theirs. The attempted hit piece failed in trying to smear my reporting, despite its use of speculation, innuendo, and omission of key context—the very tactics *The Intercept* accused me of employing.

The first thing to know about the pathetic excuse for a story is that I had no idea it was being made. Mackey, the article's author, never reached out to me for comment, even though my Twitter direct messages are open, and my email is on my author page at Townhall.com.

That's failing Journalism 101. Not following the most basic journalistic protocol for such a story, a profile of sorts, was the first red flag, especially since I am the first person targeted in the piece. I am quite literally the face for it; I am in the featured image.

How did I try to "smear" BLM? *The Intercept*'s first example was my video from Portland of Antifa rioters attacking the Democratic headquarters, along with my subsequent appearance on Laura Ingraham's show that night. This, according to Mackey, was a problem. Were it not for my footage, the affair would have remained a local story.

Of course, who is Robert Mackey to determine what should or should not be a national story? But if a violent attack on Oregon's Democratic Party headquarters to protest Joe Biden's Inauguration doesn't merit national attention, then I'm not sure what would.

The entire piece is a sloppy hash of distortions, lies, and complaints about the success of efforts by my colleagues and me to expose Antifa violence. The gist of it is summed up in the following passage:

> Rosas and [Jorge] Ventura are not household names, but it's important to understand their reporting, because they are members of an informal club of right-wing video journalists who roam from city to city, feeding the conservative media's hunger for images of destruction and violence on the margins of left-wing protests.
>
> ...The impact of their work is hard to overstate. Even as they remain relatively unknown, this tight-knit group has produced many of the most viral videos of Black Lives Matter protests over the past year. And those images have helped create the false impression, relentlessly driven home by FOX News and Republican politicians, that the nationwide wave of protests that erupted after George Floyd was killed was nothing but an excuse for mindless rioting.

Aside from the use of the term "false" in "false impression," it's actually fairly close to the mark. *The Intercept* clearly is unhappy with our success. The rest of their feature is merely a failed attempt to discredit those of us shining a spotlight on Antifa's shadowy brand of anarchy and violence. It imputes racist motives to me, and accuses my fellow Riot Squad colleagues and me of "using riot porn to incite fear in white people."

Honestly, it's worth checking out if only for the laughs.

Due to how poorly *The Intercept's* story was slapped together, it's no surprise it invited a massive and rightfully deserved backlash, and not just from conservatives. Glenn Greenwald, who founded the site but had left the publication several months earlier, called out his former colleagues for their pile of garbage.

Zaid Jilani, a former reporter at *The Intercept*, was equally forceful: "When I started at *The Intercept* in 2015, I really admired its thoughtfulness and independence. The reality is it's just a partisan outfit these days, I don't think they think they have to be fair to anyone to the right of Noam Chomsky."

Huffington Post senior justice reporter Ryan Reilly said the story had missed the mark, tweeting, "Think it's best to assess the work of reporters individually rather than lump them in with others they link up with for safety. I certainly wouldn't want to be judged by the prior or current political views of one particular media figure I worked alongside in Ferguson."[74]

The blowback clearly caught *The Intercept* off guard. The outlet reposted the story to social media and released a statement saying they stand by the report. Mackey tweeted a lengthy thread on his personal account to explain why his report was not the pile of shit it actually was.

Many of my supporters speculated that *The Intercept* was basically just trying to bring enough attention to me that I could be identified and attacked at the next riot. Mackey denied the charge, but there's probably some truth to the idea.

Again, because *The Intercept* did not reach out to me for comment, Mackey seems to be unaware I *do* have to hide my identity when I'm at riots. It's because of accusations against me like those published in *The Intercept* that I'm all for wearing a mask at riots; if someone were to find out I'm with conservative media, I doubt I would emerge unscathed.

I wrote a lengthy rebuttal to *The Intercept's* story, showing point-by-point what they got wrong. After hearing nothing from them, I emailed Mackey and Editor-in-Chief Betsy Reed asking for a comment about the flaws in the story.

In the interests of transparency, I will include Mackey's full response, though it hardly addressed any of the points I made. Still, it's worth reading as it offers a revealing look into the warped mindset of radical leftists:

> Let me answer your last question first, which is simply that I did not get in touch with you for comment because my piece was an

analysis of your published work, informed by the video you've posted online, your television appearances on FOX News and other public comments (including the 90 minute interview about your work and career you did with Kalen D'Almeida last December).

I didn't think it was necessary to speak to you about your video journalism to write an evaluation of it for the same reason that I don't think it is necessary to speak to an author to write a review of their book, or to a filmmaker to write a review of their movie. You put the work out there and I wrote about it as a critic, and argued that video you shot was used to create a false impression of the protest movement for racial justice.

That touches on the central point that I think needs to be clarified. The headline for my video report and article says precisely that your work was "used to" smear Black Lives Matter. I think the key thing that might not be clear to you is that my analysis was not mainly about your work, or individual videos you shot, but about how some video shot by you and seven of your colleagues was used by conservative media outlets to create a false impression about racial justice protesters, and to discredit their aims by focusing disproportionately on acts of violence, aggression, arson or looting on the margins of protests.

As I reported, independent researchers cited by Republican Sen. Ron Johnson as experts found that 94 percent of the protests associated with Black Lives Matter in the United States in 2020 were entirely peaceful. My piece argues that conservative media, most importantly FOX News, and Republican politicians, most importantly Trump, used your video and that of other field reporters to focus so intensely on the 6 percent of protests where there was violence, that the public got a wildly distorted view of how common violence was at the protests.

This is why your work was featured at the start of our video report: to illustrate the viral video to FOX News pipeline that I think was an important part of how conservative viewers were misled about the protest movement by the network, in part by using your video. The fact that a national news broadcast would focus on such a relatively minor incident as the trashing of the Oregon Democratic office by a handful of black bloc anarchists on Inauguration Day is a good illustration of how distorted the coverage of protests on FOX had become by then.

I also did not say that you exclusively filmed violence—and my piece includes a clip you shot of a peaceful protest in West Philadelphia—so the fact that you shared some video of peaceful protests does not undermine my analysis that you were invited on FOX News, and got the most views on Twitter, when you posted images of violence.

Finally, it is incorrect to say that my article or video insinuates that you "tried to hide the fact" that you left a protest in West Philadelphia to film looting in northern Philadelphia where there was no protest. My point was that by leaving a peaceful protest to cover looting by people who were not protesters, you and your colleagues provided video that could be used by FOX News and others to falsely accuse Black Lives Matter protesters of looting. That obviously happened, and my video report includes a clip of Tucker Carlson playing your video on-screen as he made the false claim that "more than 1,000 BLM activists–Joe Biden voters–and anarchists looted and destroyed businesses."

As I said in the introduction to my review of the coverage of the protests in Philadelphia, this was an example of how video can be used to mislead viewers because even when videographers like you and your colleagues "accurately record what they witness, their selective focus on unrest after police shootings helps conservative outlets demonize Black Lives Matter protesters." If you look at the coverage of Philadelphia that week on Tucker Carlson's show, it is clear that video of the looting was used, as I said, to "make the looting in one part of the city not the peaceful protest in another the focus of days of misleading politicized coverage on FOX."

MEDIA AFTERMATH

Robert Mackey's response was a long way of saying the main story was not *really* about me or my colleagues, but about the broader conservative ecosystem that used my videos to create a false narrative.

In his mind, I am part of the foundation of what he considers conservative propaganda. My reporting therefore needs to be discredited.

Ultimately, I think what we disagree on is how much the non-peaceful incidents during America's protests actually matter. To Mackey and *The Intercept*, the six or seven percent of protests that turned into violent riots are relatively small beer.

I disagree. Violence and mayhem and terror and destruction are real stories. They deserve to be reported when they occur. And—this is important—they need to be countered and put down, not excused by cowards and quislings. It's the way to ensure future riots won't spring up.

In the end, what was surprising about the whole situation was how such a failed hit piece had not happened sooner. I remember thinking in the fall of 2020 that I had not been called out for my reporting by a single major media outlet. There's a reason for that, of course: My reporting was truthful. It is really that simple. The fires were real. The gunfire was real. The deaths and injuries were real. The livelihoods that the riots ruined were real. And I reported the real things I saw.

But what do I know? I'm just a college dropout.

8

Democrats Care About Ordinary People

I BELIEVE the riots the nation experienced in 2020 were inevitable given the economic dislocation and job losses caused by COVID lockdowns, people being sick of staying inside all the time, the weather getting warmer, and the natural tensions produced by an upcoming presidential election. It was only a matter of time before something sparked America's powder keg.

That said, I believe that Democrats and liberals at the local, state, and even national level made the unrest worse than it needed to be.

Take the Minnesota Freedom Fund (MFF), for example. It was advertised as a bail fund to be used to help release peaceful protesters who were being wrongly arrested during the protests.

With the riots were raging, celebrities who were *not* in Minnesota tried scoring virtue signal points by publicly declaring they would be donating to the MFF. Those who donated included Seth Rogen, Steve Carrell, Nick Kroll, Josh Safdie, Ben Schwartz, Rob Delaney, Pete Holmes, Don Cheadle, and Janelle Monáe.[75]

But it wasn't just actors and actresses who gave money to rioters. At least 13 members of Joe Biden's campaign donated to the Minnesota Freedom Fund. His eventual vice-presidential pick, Kamala Harris, tweeted a link to the MFF on June 1st asking her millions of followers to "chip in now to the @MNFreedomFund to help post bail for those protesting on the ground in Minnesota."[76]

Woke corporations got in on the act as well. Lululemon, for instance, gave $100,000 to the MFF.[77]

The fund received over $30 million in the first few days of the riots alone. But it was not just peaceful protesters who were bailed out with MFF funds. Court documents showed that MFF used $75,000 to bail out Jaleel Stallings, who had been arrested for allegedly shooting at SWAT members during the riots.

The MFF also used funds to bail out individuals arrested for offenses completely unrelated to the riots. Darnika Floyd, for instance, was in jail for stabbing an acquaintance to death after a potential sexual encounter went awry. She was sprung thanks to $100,000 from MFF. The fund also paid $350,000 to bail out Christopher Boswell, a twice-convicted rapist, charged with kidnapping, assault, and sexual assault in two separate cases.

"I often don't even look at a charge when I bail someone out," Greg Lewin, the interim executive director of the fund told Fox9. "I will see it after I pay the bill because it is not the point. The point is the system we are fighting."[78]

Then there was the case of Thomas Moseley, whom the MFF bailed out not once but twice. He was arrested a third time on felony weapons and drug charges.[79]

Often lost in the media attention the Minnesota Freedom Fund received is that legitimate protesters—i.e., actual nonviolent individuals—had no need to be bailed out. If arrested, which seldom occurred, they would usually be given citations and released. (The only time I saw large numbers of nonviolent protesters being arrested in Minneapolis was when a group was rounded up for refusing to leave a highway intersection by US Bank Stadium long after curfew.)

Even MFF's Lewin admitted they probably bailed out only a few dozen actual protesters. The fact that peaceful protesters would have no use for the services of the Minnesota Freedom Fun should call into question its very existence.

When I reached out to the White House press shop to see if there was any regret for Harris sending the tweet, or if they would issue a condemnation about MFF funds going to bail out violent offenders, the White House said they had no comment. Lululemon did not respond to my request for comment either.

Not surprisingly, the fact that rioters and hardened criminals were being bailed out did not sit well with the survivors of May's riots. Some of those whom I interviewed were not even aware of what the MFF truly was and what the bail fund had done.

"That's actually really bad. It should not be this way. I mean, they should get punished so people learn and not do it again," GM Tobacco's co-owner, Shawn, told me. "I don't think they should be bailed out. That's totally wrong."

"I think it *was* a great idea but obviously it's mismanaged," said Jessica, another entrepreneur whose business near the 3rd Precinct barely escaped destruction. "Bail out the protesters, not rapists! I mean that's ridiculous! And who does that and thinks that's okay?"

One of Jessica's employees, Harold, added, "It's one of those things where maybe you're at a protest but then you get arrested and you have a warrant, or if you're a criminal, for something else, then you need to stay in jail for your other crimes."

Aaron, a business owner who closed his store in the wake of the riots, simply said what Vice President Harris did was "criminal."

Scott Carpenter's B&L Office Furniture in Kenosha was destroyed by looters. He said what happened with the money donated to the MFF "sucks." "I think a lot of people jumped on board with things, not realizing what they were jumping on board with because they saw one side; they heard one side and they didn't hear the whole story."

When Scott heard what Kamala Harris had tweeted, it "set me off." "I'm thinking, 'Are you for real?'" he said. "Not that I was crazy about our president, Donald Trump, but to me, at the moment, he was better than the other offer that I had on the table. I thought, 'If somebody agrees with something like [the MFF], man you're just letting out the evil to just reign.' You can't have that. If people are doing wrong, they need to be held accountable for it. If I did wrong, I need to be held accountable for it....I think it sucks that [Harris] was involved in helping people get out."

Kenosha businessman Jim Degrazio, whose thrift store, Treasures Within, was attacked by looters, had equally strong words for Kamala Harris. "I think what she did was wrong, just plain out wrong. How can you bail people out that are actually destroying the city? How can you back that up? Whenever somebody is breaking the law, how can you back that up and sleep at night?"

An entirely different worldview was articulated by Devin Hogan, chairman of the Minneapolis Democratic-Farmer-Labor Party, who saw no issue with the riots that terrorized the local population.

In an op-ed for a monthly community newspaper, Hogan wrote: "Like it or not, setting the Third Precinct on fire was a genuine revolutionary moment. An act of pure righteousness to open new worlds of under-standing. The people declared themselves ungovernable and unilaterally took their power back. The largest international human rights move-ment in modern history had begun. The youth of Minneapolis carried all of this. The cops started it."

When I reached out to the Minnesota Democratic-Farmer-Labor Par-ty for a comment about Hogan's writings, they pointed to an op-ed by state DFL Chair Ken Martin in which he condemned Hogan's "appall-ing" words.

It's worth noting that when that piece appeared, a month after Ho-gan's supposedly appalling comments, Hogan was still chair of the DFL's Minneapolis chapter. (He still held that position as this book went to print.)

Rep. Alexandria Ocasio-Cortez (D-NY), meanwhile, offered her own curious justification for the unrest in New York City, dismissing any connection between cuts to the New York Police Department's budget and rising crime rates.

"So why is this uptick in crime happening?" she asked during a virtual town hall event. Her theory was economic desperation due to

COVID-related record unemployment. "Maybe this has to do with the fact that people aren't paying their rent and are scared to pay their rent and so they go out and they need to feed their child, and they don't have money so...they feel like they either need to shoplift some bread or go hungry that night."

As I explained in Chapter One, the only time I could see this argument holding any weight was during the height of the riots in Minneapolis, and it could only be applied to taking staples like groceries or formula. But the looting in America's cities in 2020 was entirely different, with shopping carts being used to haul away high-end electronics and other pricey, non-essential items being the common visual in town after town. In fact, in the riots I covered *after* Minneapolis, foodstuffs were often the least looted items.

I was in Philadelphia on October 27th when unrest broke out after a police-involved shooting. I made my way to a local Walmart that I'd heard was particularly hard-hit that night. Philadelphia Police had secured the store, and because of their perimeter, I was unable to enter. The police officers guarding the Walmart then made a move to stop the looting at the stores in the nearby strip mall. In a line, they started to powerwalk over, prompting the looters to run out of the stores and go into their cars or on foot to escape. By the time the officers reached the businesses, all the looters had gotten away. Things quieted down in that portion of the parking lot, but across the big lot and the street, the businesses there, which included a Dollar Tree and a Boost T-Mobile, were being hit.

Due to there being more stores, there were more people taking part in the looting. This presented a problem since the parking lot was much smaller width-wise; drivers, in their haste to leave or pull up, were constantly crashing into each other.

When we left to go back to the first area we had arrived at, the officers had left, presumably to respond to the shootings that were taking place nearby. It did not take long for the word to spread, and looters came rushing back to finish what they had started.

Savanah Hernandez and I entered to record what was happening. I couldn't help but notice much of the grocery section was being ignored.

The food items that were disturbed, such as the strawberries and bakery items, were simply smashed on the floor.

While I was studying this scene, remarking to myself how the groceries seemed practically radioactive to looters, they moved on to ransack a nearby Lowe's Home Improvement store.

I was observing the looting of America's cities firsthand, and there was no question in my mind that it was being driven by many different motives. Trying to feed hungry children in uncertain economic times, as AOC suggested, was not one of them.

It's telling that Democrats at the national level took their time before forcefully denounce the rioting and looting. Instead, they chose to focus on—and even celebrate—the protests, while ignoring the carnage into which these protests often descended (and, of course, ignoring the victims of that carnage).

CNN host Don Lemon pointed this out in August, suggesting it could be a problem for Democrats.

"It's showing up in the polling. It's showing up in focus groups. It is the only thing right now that is sticking. The riots and the protests have become indistinguishable," Lemon said. He added, "This is a blind spot for Democrats. I think Democrats are ignoring this problem or hoping that it will go away, and it's not going to go away."

Note that Lemon wasn't calling out his ideological compatriots for dragging their feet; he was concerned that the lack of Democratic condemnation of rioting could hurt them in the November elections.[80] (Spoiler alert: He was right.)

"The President and his allies are trying to tap into that frustration and distract from his breathtaking failures by giving folks someone to blame other than them," said former First Lady Michelle Obama in a video filmed for the Biden campaign that launched on October 6th. "They're stoking fears about black and brown Americans, lying about how minorities will destroy the suburbs, whipping up violence and intimidation, and they're pinning it all on what's been an overwhelmingly peaceful movement for racial solidarity. It's true. Research backs it up. Only a tiny fraction of demonstrations have had any violence at all."

It was a master class in playing the race card. "What the President is doing," she said, is "patently false, it's morally wrong, and yes, it is racist."[81]

I found myself covering the BLM riot in the suburbs of Wauwatosa, Wisconsin *one day* later.

If anything was patently false, morally wrong, and yes, even racist, it was how the mainstream media pushed the narrative that Jacob Blake was unarmed when he was shot by Kenosha, Wisconsin, officer Rusten Sheskey in August. Working in tandem, Democrats rushed to condemn the shooting because he was "unarmed":

- "Police shot Jacob Blake, an unarmed Black man, multiple times in the back as his sons watched. I pray for Jacob's recovery. But prayers are not simply enough—we must demand accountability and justice for all Black people terrorized by police."—*Rep. Ilhan Omar (D-MN)*[82]
- "I am praying for Jacob Blake's family and his speedy recovery. No child should ever have to witness their unarmed father shot in the back. This shooting must be investigated. #BlackLivesMatter—today, tomorrow, and every day."—*Rep. Eric Swalwell (D-CA)*[83]

- "Yesterday in Wisconsin, a police officer shot Jacob Blake, an unarmed Black man, a father, 7 times in the back. I am deeply disturbed by the video capturing part of the incident. I urge civil & criminal authorities to pursue an immediate & thorough investigation of the shooting."—*Chicago Mayor Lori Lightfoot (D)*[84]
- "The George Floyd #JusticeInPolicing Act has been sitting on Sen. McConnell's desk for two months now. And just this week, America watched as yet another unarmed Black man—Jacob Blake—was shot by police. @senatemajldr, the time for action is now. Let us vote on this bill."—*Sen. Dick Durbin (D-IL)*[85]

The only problem is that Blake *was* armed, which factored into the prosecutor's ultimate decision to not charge Sheskey for shooting Blake.

So what explains this seemingly willful decision to misrepresent one of the most salient facts about the Jacob Blake incident?

In a word—politics.

The main issue was that in an election year, Democrats did not want to alienate the mostly youthful voting bloc that was attracted to the Black Lives Matter movement. And if there's anyone who wanted to ensure people focused on the protests, and not the riots that often sprang from said protests, it was the BLM *movement*. This is not to say the *official* organization provided cover for riots, and certainly not to say peaceful protests didn't happen. But there were plenty of instances I witnessed where BLM movement protests started out peacefully but then devolved into violent riots.

From what I saw, some of the peaceful protesters were fine when agitators within the crowd took their "direct action." Often when buildings were damaged or police officers were attacked, they would chant, "What did you see? We ain't see shit!"

And don't forget the representative from the Chicago BLM chapter who said, "I don't care if someone decides to loot a Gucci or a Macy's or a Nike store, because that makes sure that person eats" because, among other factors, these businesses have insurance."[86]

As with other cases of rioting, the problem is it was not only big corporations who were targeted. Or even for-profit businesses. During the August riots in Chicago, rioters smashed the windows of the Ronald McDonald House, a charity that helps families with very sick children.

Families inside the building said they were unable to leave due to the situation in the streets being too dangerous.[87] It seemed as if rioters were simply bent on destruction, no matter the target.

When I emailed the BLM Chicago chapter and the Black Lives Matter Global Network to ask if they stood by their representative's remarks, neither responded to my requests for comment.

The "businesses have insurance" mindset explains why so many protesters were fine with the rioters kicking business owners and their employees while they were down.

Many of them, oddly, drew the line at attacking private homes.

Unfortunately, that line of thinking did not exactly extend to Kenosha, where apartments that sat above businesses that had been set on fire did not escape the flames. *The New York Times* reported families living in these apartments were able to get out just in time, though some of their pets were burned alive.[88]

Liberals and progressives often point to a Princeton University study that concluded 93 percent of all demonstrations associated with the BLM movement were peaceful. On its face, "93 percent" may sound pretty good, but between May 24th and August 22nd, there were over 500 violent demonstrations in 220 locations in the United States. That averages to about six violent demonstrations per day.

The 7 percent is used to dismiss the nationwide damage that cost over $2 billion and resulted in at least 20 deaths. Furthermore, it's worth noting the study's cutoff date is right before the Kenosha riots.[89]

In no sane world is such a high number of riots in a short amount of time acceptable or sustainable for any country. We're not talking about 500 violent events over the course of 10 years or even one year, we're talking about three months. Frankly, it only takes one riot to massively set back a community already struggling from the effects of COVID-19 lockdowns. Now multiply that effect to more than 500 violent incidents in cities and towns across the United States.

The "autonomous zones" that popped up in Seattle, Portland, and other parts of the country were only able to exist because the Democrat-controlled city governments allowed them. The longer they went on, the more likely people were to get hurt or killed.

Let's revisit CHAZ, where Mayor Durkan told CNN's Chris Cuomo she did not know how long she would let the occupation last, but who knows?

The city could have a "summer of love" in CHAZ.

All it took was one day being on the ground to see that the CHAZ "summer of love" was not going to happen.

To make matters worse, even *after* the multiple crimes that were committed in and around CHAZ/CHOP during its brief existence, Durkan appeared on MSNBC to provide a "reality check" after South Dakota Gov. Kristi Noem turned a spotlight on America's urban riots during her address to the Republican National Convention.

"Her caricature of the great cities across America is not only wrong, it's purposefully wrong," Durkan said, ludicrously. "I think she needs to get off Twitter and get off FOX News and come see our city." (In another life-comes-at-you-fast moment, during a riot in Seattle two weeks later, rioters threw Molotov cocktails at Seattle Police officers.[90] Good thing for Mayor Durkan that Gov. Noem didn't take her up on the offer to visit Seattle then.)

Durkan's decision to bend the knee to the mob, to allow them their own police-free zone, almost certainly resulted in deaths and crimes being committed that could have been avoided.

When Seattle officials finally moved in to re-take the zone, Seattle Police had little trouble pushing the occupiers out. It would have been far better if they had done it during the first week of the CHAZ experiment.

A lesser-known "autonomous zone" was created in Atlanta, Georgia, following the police-involved death of Rayshard Brooks. Brooks was killed on June 12th after Atlanta police arrived at Wendy's in response to a 911 call about a man passed out in a drive-through lane.

When police arrived, Brooks appeared intoxicated. Officers tried handcuffing and arresting him for DUI. In videos from that night, Brooks at first cooperated with the officers, but he then tried to fight them off. He managed to steal a taser from one of the officers and appeared to try to use it on police while trying to get away. That's when Officer Devin Brosnan shot Brooks.[91]

The country was still reeling from the riots in the aftermath of George Floyd's death, and Atlanta looked like the next hotspot. Rumors spread there would be a big strike among the Atlanta Police Department after the district attorney charged Brosnan and another officer for the death of Brooks. I figured I needed to be in Atlanta.

The Wendy's where the incident occurred was set ablaze by protesters the night after the shooting. A CHAZ-like atmosphere developed. Protesters set up roadblocks, guarding the small area with firearms. While it did not make headlines for being an "autonomous zone"—its occupiers did not advertise it as such—it was operated in much the same way.

The first thing I saw when I arrived was a confrontation between the protesters and a white couple in a pickup truck. The crowd was blocking the truck, forcing it to turn around, but not before some in the crowd had grown hostile and smashed one of the vehicle's windows. The driver yelled he would come back with a gun as he sped away.

Occasionally Atlanta police came around, but they were always chased away by occupiers. Much like in CHAZ, the area felt like a block party at first, in part because it coincided with the Juneteenth holiday.

However, the atmosphere turned dangerous after dark. Multiple shootings took place in the area during the first week, with at least one young woman being hit. A black man using his phone to livestream on Facebook was attacked, taking a punch to the back of the head by occupiers who did not want anybody to film.

I was with Jorge Ventura on my last night in Atlanta. Tensions clearly were rising, and everyone was suspicious. At one point, two young men with guns walked up and asked us our thoughts about what was happening.

We were trying to be respectful and said we were getting ready to leave. They asked if we had seen the memorial people had created in Brooks' memory. We had, we told them, and again said we needed to go home for the night. The men insisted we see the memorial again and offered to provide us with an "armed escort." I did not want to go down to the Wendy's; it was pitch black and felt too dangerous. But no matter what we told them, they said we needed to go with them. Feeling as if we had no other choice, we obliged.

Everything was going well as we nervously approached the memorial until another group of occupiers said they recognized us from earlier. They said they had told us to leave and were very suspicious we were back. Their hostility grew. Some accused us of being undercover officers.

I said we were more than happy to leave and not come back. After a few more tense moments, our two armed escorts decided to usher Jorge and me out of the area. They told us if we wanted to prove we were not undercover cops, then we had to come back tomorrow during daylight, adding if we did not come back during the day and we were caught being around during the nighttime, then there would be problems.

What was clear after over a hundred days of rioting in cities across America was how the almost universally Democratic leadership in those locales allowed the riots to happen. Particularly galling were the decisions made by many local district attorneys to refuse to prosecute those who were arrested by the police for rioting.

I asked the former Acting Secretary of the U.S. Department of Homeland Security, Chad Wolf, about this. He was enemy number two in the eyes of the Democrats and the media (after President Trump), since he was at the helm of DHS during the riots at the federal courthouse in Portland.

Wolf told me his agency had been monitoring Portland and other cities as the riots continued into June. Towards the end of June and the beginning of July, he said the Federal Protective Service in Portland notified them that the demonstrations were becoming more violent and "sophisticated," and that they would not be able to protect the Mark O. Hatfield courthouse with the resources they had. This led to DHS sending reinforcements to Portland after July 4th.

Wolf said he contacted both Oregon Gov. Kate Brown and Portland Mayor Ted Wheeler to offer additional resources to the Oregon State Police and Portland Police Bureau to help deal with the nightly riots.

"I made it clear to both the Mayor and the Governor that we wanted local police, local officials to deal with that," Wolf told me. He said DHS "would provide assistance to them, so if they didn't need more people, that's fine, but if they needed more intelligence, more assets, whatever they needed, the Department was ready to provide that to them in order to bring this to a close."

Instead of accepting DHS' offer for help, Wolf said, both Wheeler and Brown blamed his officers for the repeated violence in the city.

"They're saying law enforcement is the reason that there's violence at the courthouse, which is just absolutely insane," Wolf said. "It's insane that we're supposed to, in their minds, stand by and watch the courthouse be defaced night after night after night, and if we somehow protect that courthouse then we are inciting violence."

After blaming his officers for the riots, Wolf said Brown and Wheeler demanded he remove *all* federal officers from the courthouse.

"So that was the message that they sent me in early July. I told them I couldn't do that; I wasn't going to not do my job. We needed to protect the courthouse, and we wanted to do that in partnership with them."

Making the situation worse, and more dangerous, according to Sec. Wolf, was an order from the Portland City Council forcing the Portland Police not to communicate with or coordinate with federal assets.

"In their mind, DHS was the cause for this violent activity and that if they stopped talking to us that we would then somehow go away, and the violence would stop," he said. "Of course, we knew that to be a joke; we knew that not to be the case and history has proven that." Wolf pointed out that riots continued in different areas of the city even after DHS pulled its extra officers in early August.

It's also worth mentioning that according to the Portland Police Bureau's timeline of protests, city officials declared a riot 15 different times in the month of August in areas *away* from the federal courthouse.[92] Surely federal officers, who were not present in those situations, were not responsible for the violence Portland experienced in those locations.

"If you don't hold these folks accountable, and you just let them do this, they're just going to keep doing it, so yeah there was a lot of frustration."

During the month of July when Portland was the national story, Wolf said there was an elevated "threat environment" around him and his family, with increased death threats and protesters showing up almost every weekend to his home in Alexandria, Virginia. The "threat environment," he said, was the result of the false narratives coming from Democrats and the media.

"One of the most troubling things, from my perspective, was just the dishonesty we saw from a lot in the media and a lot of political policy makers and others back here in DC," Wolf told me. "In my mind, they intentionally confused the American public by saying these are peaceful protesters. So then you have a view that the federal government is somehow squashing individuals' ability to do just that, peacefully protest. That wasn't the case at all."

Wolf also noted how protests often were peaceful during the day without DHS officers needing to respond. They usually had to come out in force at night after rioters started to attack the federal building under cover of darkness.

"I think there's some [valid] criticism; there was some things we could have done better," Wolf said. "But none of it was illegal. None of it was outside the scope of our responsibility. It's what we do; it's what Congress told us to do, and we did it. And members of Congress then decided, 'Well, I don't think we want you to do that now.' Well that's not how the system works."

Fearing more riots could break out, businesses in cities across the country boarded up their windows and doors as Election Day drew near. According to liberals, people were fearful because the riots that had taken place during the summer were Donald Trump's fault. The implicit threat, of course, was that there would be violence if Trump won re-election.

I want to be very clear: When I was outside the White House on election night, I brought my full kit with me. It included my armor plate carrier, gas mask, ballistic helmet, athletic cup, and first aid kit. I had all of this with me because I was expecting violence from Biden supporters (or, at least, Trump haters) if the result showed Trump projected as the winner.

Meanwhile I had zero concerns about Trump supporters appearing out of nowhere and rioting in deep blue DC (or any other part of the country, frankly) if it looked like Biden might win.

To prove this point, once Biden was declared the winner the following Saturday, street parties broke out instead of riots (with COVID-19 conveniently no longer an issue, apparently). Sadly, that changed on January 6th.

Most of the 2020 unrest occurred in Democratic strongholds, and the leaders were the ones who often failed to take the necessary steps to put down the *violent* gatherings until it got so out of control that it required help from the military.

I dedicate so many pages here to criticizing Democrats and the mainstream media because, unlike Donald Trump, they hope to get away with fanning the flames that torched whole sections of cities across America. We can't let them. It's important to highlight their hypocrisy and their failure to condemn the riots. What, after all, is the explanation for House Democrats unanimously voting to block a resolution on June 25th that condemned the rioting, including the "deliberate targeting of law enforcement officers"?[93]

Shortly after the George Floyd murder, when riots occurred outside the White House, a building that houses the leader of one of the branches of the U.S. government, there was none of the grave concern from Democrats bemoaning the assault on our democracy that they offered on January 6th.

Yet it was extraordinarily violent. A video released by the U.S. Department of the Interior, which oversees the U.S. Park Police, showed agitators throwing bricks, glass, bottles, and other projectiles at law enforcement officers. More than 60 U.S. Park Police officers were injured in the riots outside the White House.

According to a statement from the U.S. Secret Service: "Some demonstrators repeatedly attempted to knock over security barriers, and vandalized six Secret Service vehicles. Between Friday night and Sunday morning, more than 60 Secret Service Uniformed Division Officers and Special Agents sustained multiple injuries from projectiles such as bricks, rocks, bottles, fireworks, and other items. Secret Service personnel were also directly physically assaulted as they were kicked, punched, and exposed to bodily fluids. A total of 11 injured employees were transported to a local hospital and treated for non-life threating injuries."

Those are pretty straightforward descriptions of behavior any reasonable person would describe as rioting.

Yet the media took pains to avoid using the term. For instance, this is how Reuters described what happened in a tweet: "Protesters set fires near the White House in Washington, DC, the smoke mixing with billowing clouds of tear gas as police sought to clear them from the area." The word "riot" does not appear once in the story linked to the tweet.

The violence grew so intense that the Secret Service felt compelled to rush President Trump to safety in the White House bunker. Naturally, Democrats and the media mocked Trump as if he were cowardly hiding from peaceful protesters.

- "Mr. Tough Guy was whisked into a panic bunker on Friday, as crowds assembled outside the White House. It took three-and-a-half years, but he finally got a massive crowd to show up for him in DC"—*late night television show Jimmy Kimmel*
- "It's time to take action. It is time to stand up...not hide behind fences or in a bunker. Now is the time. Instead, this president...is literally and figuratively in a bunker"—*CNN host Don Lemon*

- "Why does Donald Trump need a bunker when he has thoughts and prayers?"—*gun control activist David Hogg*
- "Remember, this is the same president, who went down and hid in a bunker at a time when, you know, the police forces that he ordered were firing tear gas on peaceful protests"—*Sen. Tammy Duckworth (D-IL)*
- "Make us all safe. Go back to your bunker. #BlackLivesMatter" —*Seattle Mayor Jenny Durkan*
- "Given his bone spurs, it must have been very painful to be rushed down to a bunker. You could almost give him props for being willing to undergo that pain"—*CNN host Anderson Cooper*

White House staff who worked in the Trump administration during this turbulent time saw first hand how the environment in Washington, D.C. had changed for the worse over time.

One former staffer told me there was "heightened concerned" among the Trump workforce that the White House would be a main target when the riots in the Twin Cities first started.

"As a staffer who would take the Metro occasionally, walking out of the White House grounds sometimes was a little nerve-wracking because you never really knew who was going to accost you," they said, adding even though they would make sure to stash their pass when they left the complex, it was still obvious where they were coming from since they were one of the few people who was going into the office during the COVID lockdowns in the spring.

In the immediate aftermath of the White House being attacked by BLM rioters, getting to and leaving from the grounds changed for people who still had to go to the building, especially since a large metal fence was erected.

"What was a beautiful area now just looked like a fort...You started to build a relationship with the Secret Service men and women. [They're] amazing patriots, and they just looked run down. And hearing stories of their friends getting hit on the head, it was really a sad time to see people that you would see day-to-day always being on edge and not knowing when they would have to spring into action again."

The former Trump staffer, who went on to work on Capitol Hill and was present during the January 6th riot, said it was "dumbfounding" to see the different reactions the mainstream media and Democrats had to the two events. The source said in their experience with mainstream D.C. reporters, "a lot of these people are just actors at the end of day," who would behave much differently once the cameras stopped rolling.

"Not all of these people were terrible people, but they even mentioned to me many times they had a job to do, which is disgusting in its own right...and that job is to perpetuate narratives that gain clicks and gain attention that will end up putting their opposition in a worse position."

They acknowledged the January 6th riot was wrong and should not have happened, but once it was over, they had zero concerns for their safety going to the Capitol building, which was something they did not feel when they worked at the White House in 2020.

"It is crazy to think that people genuinely believe...that January 6th was this big event that completely changed the lives of everyone in the world and on Capitol Hill" or believe it was worse than 9/11 and the Civil War, they said, noting for them, the constant stress of 2020's multiple riots, protests, and threats of riots in Washington, D.C. was more of a drain "mentally and physically" than the aftermath of the Capitol riot.

There's no question we are living through polarized political times. The Capitol riot accomplished nothing to solve our nation's troubles. It only gave Democrats and their media allies the hammer they had been looking for to wield against their political adversaries, especially those who were not in Washington, DC on January 6th. The pro-Trump rioters' rage blinded them to recognizing the consequences their actions would have. Regardless of the fact that Trump never told supporters to go inside the Capitol, or that he did release a video telling rioters to go home, the damage was already done.

POLITICAL AFTERMATH

It's ironic that President Trump received condemnation for encouraging a violent riot when, in fact, the evidence shows he did no such thing. After all, there actually *were* prominent Democrats who actively encouraged rioting and violence during the civil unrest of 2020.

The most clear-cut example comes courtesy of radical California Congresswoman Maxine Waters, who travelled to Minnesota to stir up agitation after an accidental shooting by a police officer in Brooklyn Center, Minnesota. When suspect Daunte Wright resisted arrest after being pulled over, Officer Kimberly Potter shot him with her gun. She had meant to use her taser.

Several nights of riots broke out as a result. Raising tensions further was the fact that Derek Chauvin's trial for the death of George Floyd was winding down nearby in Minneapolis. The whole country was anxiously awaiting a resolution in that case.

Enter Rep. Waters to try to throw gasoline on the fires. Asked what people should do if Chauvin ended up not being convicted, she replied, "I know this; we've got to stay in the streets. We've got to demand justice."

"She added, "We are looking for a guilty verdict.... If nothing does not happen then, we know, we have got to not only stay in the streets but we have to fight for justice. I am very hopeful, and I hope that we are going to get a verdict that says 'guilty, guilty, guilty,' and if we don't, we cannot go away," she said, adding, "We have got to get more confrontational."

She later wrote an op-ed trying to clean up her words, but it seemed pretty clear cut what she wanted to happen—what she was threatening would happen—if a jury found Chauvin not guilty on the charges he faced.

Rep. Waters' call for violence perhaps wasn't all that surprising considering her history of making incendiary comments. That's her nature. Something else that appears to be in her nature is hypocrisy. Ahead of her trip to the Minneapolis area to denounce police and call for further violence, her office sought a police escort.[94]

9

BLM Cares About the Black Community and Wokeness of COVID

IRONIES abounded during the 2020 riots. One is that the police officers who often found themselves under attack in the mayhem that purported to be about racial justice were, themselves, people of color.

Another is that many of those business owners and entrepreneurs whose stores and businesses were looted or even destroyed were also minorities.

The official Black Lives Matter organization, indeed the movement as a whole, supposedly exists to prevent the death of or harm to minorities at the hands of police. But so often it was those same minority populations that were harmed—in some cases even killed—when supposedly well-meaning and sincere protests morphed into bedlam and turmoil. The situation was often exacerbated by police departments that were understaffed and overwhelmed or, in too many cases, undercut by faint-hearted governors, mayors, and city council members.

In the aftermath of the riots, BLM faces an uphill battle because of the increase in violent crime in major American cities. *The Wall Street Journal*'s Kimberly Strassel nicely summed up the scope of this problem in a column in November 2021: "The violence that the left egged on in the wake of George Floyd's murder has only grown. Nationally, homicides increased by 30% from 2019 to 2020. Chicago is likely to end 2021 with its highest murder rate in 25 years. Portland, Ore., home to routine violent riots, is on track to surpass 1,200 shootings this year, compared with 400 in 2019. Los Angeles recorded more homicides in July than in any month for more than a decade."

It is no surprise, therefore, that residents do not want to see a decrease in police budgets or a decrease in policing as a whole.

A Gallup poll published on August 5, 2020 showed when asked, "Would you rather the police spend more time, the same amount of time or less time as they currently spend in your area?" More than 60 percent of black Americans said they want police presence to remain the same. Only 19 percent of black Americans said they want fewer police officers in their area.[95]

That sentiment appears to have not gone away nearly a year later. A *USA Today*/Suffolk University/*Detroit Free Press* poll found that, by an overwhelming margin, Detroit residents are more concerned about public safety than police reform.[96] Black residents ranked crime at the top of their list of concerns: 24 percent cited public safety, with only 3 percent naming police reform. Funny enough, white residents were more concerned about police reform (12 percent) than public safety (10 percent).

Now, I'm not a gambling man, but I would bet the greater concern over public safety is due to Detroit seeing 16 more homicides (186) at the time of this writing in July 2021 than at the same point a year earlier.

The only thing the BLM movement and organization have going for them is the widely held belief, at least among self-described Democratic voters, that police kill hundreds of unarmed black people a year.

This is not meant to minimize deaths at the hands of police. But it is easy to call for the defunding of police departments when people believe that thousands of black people are killed every year. In 2019, the actual total number was 235. As for shootings of *unarmed* blacks, *The Washington Post*'s database of police shootings shows that police fatally shot 13 unarmed black people in 2019.

Defunding police departments in order to combat racism is in the same vein of overreaction as giving the federal government vast surveillance powers in the aftermath of 9/11 or banning AR-15s after mass shootings. Just because it sounds like the "right" thing to do doesn't mean it is the solution.

This was what frustrated me most about people downplaying the riots. The criminal element sees how it can use the current political climate, specifically the attitude towards policing, for its benefit long after the un-rest is over.

I saw the effects of a badgered police force when I went on a ride-along with a Washington Metro Police detective in the southeast portion of the city, where a simple trip across the 11th Street Bridge revealed a wholly different operational environment.

After entering the Metro Police's 7th District station, I was given a rundown on the manpower problems they were having. They were down 100 officers from what they're supposed to have. The station was also supposed to have at least 40 detectives, but they were down to 23 and two more had put in their papers to leave the department that week. When it was time to leave to tour the southeast, I was shown how many squad cars were not being used.

"Before, we didn't have enough cars for everyone," a detective told me. "Now we don't have the bodies to fill them." As we were about to leave, we heard the unmistakable sound of gunfire right down the street from us. Around 10 to 15 shots were fired. We later found out one person was hit and two guns, a rifle, and a handgun were recovered from the scene.

While driving around neighborhoods in southeast DC, the detective said the situation had started to deteriorate around 2015, but the riots and rhetoric around police had exacerbated the problems the department was already facing.

Due to the shortage in manpower, they cannot carry out proactive po-licing like they had before. The department was forced to put a squad car, oftentimes with only one officer, in intersections near shooting hotspots. They know shootings will still take place; this way they're already on the scene to respond. But what they aren't doing is taking steps to prevent shootings before they occur.

The detective pointed to how people just hang around all day on the streets, which the officers tried to discourage in the past when there were more officers. Drug use is practiced in broad daylight, sometimes with an officer right down the street. The fear of being arrested and punished for any law-breaking had disappeared almost entirely. Perhaps the most chilling sign of the times was when we drove by a large park. It was towards the late afternoon, not too hot or humid, with the park offering plenty of shade. No one was in the park.

Since the official BLM organization received donations totaling in the millions, its leaders have been exposed as nothing more than opportunistic, Marxist charlatans. There is no better evidence for this than the fact many of those involved at the local chapter level have leveled accusations against BLM higher-ups for giving little to no funding to aid efforts on the ground.

The local BLM chapters were not immune to criticisms that were often aimed at the national organization from the people they were supposed to help. Tamika Palmer, the mother of Breonna Taylor, posted to Facebook about the Louisville BLM chapter and how she "personally have found them to be [a] fraud."

In St. Paul, Rashad Turner, the founder of the city's BLM chapter, explained why he left the organization: "I believed the organization stood for exactly what the name implies, black lives do matter. However, after a year on the inside, I learned they had little concern for rebuilding black families, and they cared even less about improving the quality of education for students in Minneapolis. That was made clear when they publicly denounced charter schools alongside the teachers union. I was an insider in Black Lives Matter. And I learned the ugly truth."[97]

Local BLM chapters have accused the main organization of not properly distributing the large sums of money the official BLM group had received in donations in 2020.

On the ground for so many different riots and BLM protests, I saw countless examples of racism being perfectly acceptable, so long as it was directed at the right target.

A prime example occurred after I flew back to Washington, D.C. from Atlanta on June 22nd. Shortly after landing, I saw on Twitter that protesters were trying to create the "Black House Autonomous Zone"—

or BHAZ—near Lafayette Square right across the street from the White House. (Doesn't quite roll off the tongue like CHAZ, but whatever.) During the establishment of BHAZ, rioters tried to tear down the iconic statue of President Andrew Jackson at the center of the square.

Secret Service, US Park Police, and the DC Metro Police pushed everyone out of the park to prevent the statue from being pulled down. Law enforcement established a line of officers right outside the park, using pepper spray to keep rioters at bay.

I happened upon a scene where a shirtless white man, complete with a man bun tied tightly on his head, had gotten in the face of a black officer. The agitator was angry because the officer had shoved him to the ground—after the man put his hands on the officer.

"I feel sorry for your family," the man screamed at the officer, spit flying in his face. "You're a piece of shit. You're a piece of shit. You really are....You're part of the fucking problem, and I hope to fuck that your children treat you the way you deserve to be treated." When another officer told the agitator to step back, he replied, "Tell this bitch ass nigga to stop putting his hands on people."

A few days later, I discovered that very same man was wanted by US Park Police and the FBI for vandalizing federal property at Lafayette Square.[98]

That was far from the only time such an incident took place.

In New York City, I saw a black transgender woman rant at a black NYPD officer, calling him a "traitor" and "black Judas," adding how he was more educated than the officer.

I frequently saw protesters single out minority officers to deride them as race traitors. Or they used vicious racial slurs. How hurling racial slurs at minority officers advances the cause of said minorities' lives mattering was lost on me. Apparently Black and Brown Lives Matter right up until the moment they are cops helping quell a riot.

CHAZ/CHOP also had its weird racial moments where discrimination was acceptable because, one assumes, it was done with good intentions.

When the Juneteenth holiday rolled around, activists in CHAZ/CHOP organized a "Juneteenth Blackout," which according to organizers meant the need for "both policy and systemic change to our systems and healing space for black people."

They explained: "What we need from our non-black allies are donations of money and supplies and the willingness to support by quietly protecting sacred space for black healing. We need allies on the outskirts who are willing to be a physical barrier of protection and to peacefully deter potential interruptions."

Roughly translated, they were calling for the formation of a segregated space just for black people. Forget that the Civil Rights movement of the 1950s and 1960s grew up to fight the evils of segregation; in Seattle segregation now was permissible—admirable, even—because social justice or something. Video posted on Twitter showed white people creating a human "wall" to mark where the black-only section started.[99]

It was also interesting to see how BLM movement protesters and rioters thought that taking violent action towards officers or innocent business owners might help achieve their dream of demilitarizing or abolishing police departments. The irony, of course, is that it took enhanced militarization—with officers and tactical gear and armored Bearcats—for law and order to be restored to America's destroyed neighborhoods.

Meanwhile, there were plenty of times where BLM or Abolish-the-Police protesters actually *did* want the police to do their jobs, despite protesters' public posture.

I saw a group of Trump supporters in Washington for a "Stop the Steal" march shortly after the November election attempt to tear down Black Lives Matter and anti-Trump signs from fences at Lafayette Square. This enraged BLM supporters, who demanded that the same police officers at whom they'd been screaming moments before arrest the right-wing offenders.

Now, I'm not sure why they were so upset at some signs—that is to say, someone else's personal property—being destroyed. I had been assured by many a BLM protestor that personal property is replaceable, and, anyway, that's what insurance is for.

It must be admitted that police provided their fair share of examples of being overly aggressive when it was not needed. The rubber bullet I was hit with is my most personal example. In many other cases, excessive force or gratuitous action from police officers backfired and was used to justify the anger and hatred towards them.

Fellow journalists Shelby Talcott and Jorge Ventura were arrested by Louisville Metro Police cracking down on protesters. It's understandable police needed to detain people who were out past curfew and were still rioting, but Shelby and Jorge were processed and booked into jail even after police confirmed they were reporters, not violent agitators (not to mention the curfew order did not apply to the media).

In Wauwatosa, Shelby and another colleague, Richie McGinnis, were beaten by officers despite following their orders to lie prone on the ground. They were in handcuffs before someone smarter came along and let them go after confirming they were press members. Independent reporter Brendan Gutenschwager was not so lucky. He was taken to jail and charged.

I understand these mistakes occurred when stress and emotions were running high. These were dangerous situations we were venturing into, and obviously arrests or near-arrests would not have happened to us if we had not been there. That said, it was our Constitutional right to be out there covering these major incidents as members of the press.

In my own case, I put some of the blame on the rioters for creating the situation where police felt they had to respond with less-than-lethal ordnance. Up until that point, the state police and National Guardsmen were merely standing around. They only reacted—and overreacted in my case, clearly—after they were attacked.

That is not to say the Antifa, Black Bloc, and progressive activists are friends of ours either. I routinely make a point to hide my identity when in the field because, had protesters/rioters known who I was, they wouldn't have hesitated to try to prevent me from doing my job. Wading among rioters and activists who were causing harm and destruction, I had no doubt I would be in great danger had my identity been known.

It's because journalists have certain legal protections that rioters and protesters occasionally label themselves as "press" but engage in antagonistic and violent behavior. When police respond in force to their mayhem, they scream they are in the media. It makes both real journalists' and the police's jobs that much harder (which, of course, is the point).

During the January 6th riot, it was both ironic and disheartening to see people who had waved "Thin Blue Line" flags or professed to "back the Blue" during the summer of 2020 attack the officers protecting the Capitol. They rationalized this by accusing the officers of betraying their oaths to the Constitution. They were "traitors."

The simple fact is the officers were doing their duty at a time when those rioting were in the wrong. It was no different from when BLM supporters and Antifa ravaged America's cities the previous summer.

In addition to the urban riots of 2020, the other big story that year, of course, was the COVID-19 pandemic. They overlapped in some curious ways.

Perhaps the biggest examples of irony, and outright hypocrisy, from the riots and protests came from those who smeared others who opposed the hard COVID-19 lockdowns as people who wanted to kill grandma with the virus.

We were told we must stay home and avoid in-person gatherings to prevent the spread of COVID-19. Countless businesses were forced to close their doors. People lost jobs and couldn't pay their bills. Playgrounds were shuttered. Church services were forbidden. Far from just being an inconvenience, many people's lives and livelihoods were shattered by harsh government edicts to stop conducting many of the basic activities of our day-to-day lives. At the heart of this was the idea that everyone had to stay distanced from virtually everyone else. Any crowd of more than a handful of people could spread the deadly virus.

All of the rhetoric came with an asterisk following George Floyd's murder. Black Lives Matter protests and Biden victory street parties that measured in the thousands were perfectly acceptable, even encouraged.

The hypocrisy came from your typical suspects, Democrats and the mainstream media.

I was never the one to tell people to wear a mask at all times or not to travel. After all, I traveled around the country during the height of the coronavirus pandemic to cover the various riots. Frankly, I'm glad masks were a thing since it made it easier to hide my identity while I was covering violent demonstrations.

Still, the utter shamelessness of Democratic officeholders when it came to refusing to wear masks or social distancing while imposing rules on everyone else (except social justice protesters, of course) should make anyone angry. Some of the nation's most prominent elected Democratic officials, such as Michigan Gov. Gretchen Whitmer, New Jersey Gov. Phil Murphy, and Los Angeles Mayor Eric Garcetti all marched maskless with BLM protesters despite advocating strict masking and social-distancing requirements for average citizens. Similarly, Chicago's mayor, Lori Lightfoot, celebrated with her mask down among a packed crowd at a Biden election victory party on November 7th.

Needless to say, no prominent Democrats or mainstream media personalities expressed concern about possible coronavirus spread at packed BLM protests during the summer. That didn't stop many, however, from scolding Republicans who packed, "shoulder to shoulder" at the White House for President Trump's Republican Convention speech on August 28. In their telling, it was reckless and "concerning."

The examples piled up as time went on, but Democrats' and the media's hypocrisy was particularly galling when holidays that are occasions for family and social get-togethers approached:

- "We're going to have to celebrate differently this year. Everyone should cancel plans with others for the 4th of July. You shouldn't gather with anyone who doesn't live in your household. Please stay home and save lives—it's that simple."—*Los Angeles Mayor Eric Garcetti, July 3rd*
- "A Stay-at-Home Advisory for Chicago will go into effect on Monday, November 16th at 6:00 a.m. This advisory calls on all Chicagoans to do the following…Stay home unless for essential reasons. Stop having guests over—including family members you do not live with. Avoid non-essential travel. Cancel traditional Thanksgiving plans."—*Chicago Mayor Lori Lightfoot announcement, November 12th*
- "We're urging everybody to keep their Thanksgiving plans as small as possible because we know that indoor gatherings and homes are particularly dangerous places for COVID-19 to spread. The smaller the gathering is, the less likely it is that someone is infected and puts their loved ones at risk. It is that simple."—*New Jersey Gov. Phil Murphy, November 16th*
- "This is hard, but making difficult sacrifices now will save lives. This Thanksgiving, keep it small. Uninvite them."—*video from Oregon Gov. Kate Brown, November 24th*
- "As the weather grows colder, we must continue to listen to medical experts and join forces to fight COVID-19…Last week out state health department director issued an epidemic order that limits indoor gatherings where COVID-19 can easily spread…If you're planning to spend Thanksgiving with people outside your household, I urge you to reconsider."—*Michigan Gov. Gretchen Whitmer, November 24th*[100]

I couldn't care less what Democratic politicians and the media had to say about not traveling to see my family for Thanksgiving and Christmas, especially since many local and state Democrats routinely were caught violating their own stay-at-home orders during the holidays.

According to the Heritage Foundation's *COVID Hypocrisy: Policymakers Breaking Their Own Rules* report, there have been at least 80 known instances since March of 2020 where Democrats did not follow the very COVID rules they advocated for. The best-known example was California Governor Gavin Newsom's dinner with friends indoors at the uber-posh Napa Valley restaurant French Laundry, a clear violation of his administration's protocols limiting social interaction.

As of this writing, the latest example was September 11, 2021, when Rep. Susie Lee (D-NV) attended a costume party in Las Vegas without a mask one day after a mask mandate went into effect.

"But Julio," you might counter, "the BLM protests were the ones that had people wearing masks."

It is true there was a much higher percentage of people wearing masks at those types of protests and riots. But that was not always the case. Anecdotally, I can say I lost count of the number of protesters who wore their masks incorrectly. It was not uncommon to see people take off their mask or pull them down to speak or shout when other people were well within six feet. I saw drum circles with maskless people dancing close together as in a nightclub, or getting right in police officers' faces to confront them while not wearing masks or wearing them improperly.

Now, I am aware of studies that concluded that mass protests did not contribute to a rise of COVID-19 positive cases. I'm skeptical about the methodology of some of them. Regardless, however, they would seem to undermine many arbitrary government edicts forbidding various social gatherings, like when Los Angeles banned outdoor dining, or numerous prohibitions against gathering for church services (including funerals).

Today, we have the knowledge that COVID-19 is extremely hard to spread outdoors. At the time when Democrats and the mainstream media routinely were excusing large gatherings, however, that had not been established. So which was it? Was COVID-19 a super deadly virus that required drastic measures to be taken, such as destroying small businesses and harming children's futures by not having in-person teaching? Or were mass events okay as long as you were gathering for righteousness, to protest injustice, or to celebrate Joe Biden's victory? According to Democrats and the mainstream media, it all depended on your politics.

Even some medical professionals wanted it both ways. A few acknowledge they had criticized anti-lockdown protests while fully supporting large BLM gatherings.[101] Like everyone else, I was concerned about COVID-19 in the early days and weeks and months. Initially, I took very seriously what medical professionals like Dr. Anthony Fauci were telling us in their press conferences and media appearances. But as time went on, it was clear the scientific community's politics made them fine with being hypocrites. They lost credibility with me and with the American public. Either we're in a pandemic or we're not, you can't have it both ways.

COVID AFTERMATH

As this chapter reveals, hypocrisy was the norm for media and prominent Democrats when it came to large demonstrations.

The Reuters twitter feed, in particular, was always good for a few laughs on that score.

"#BlackLivesMatter protesters march through central London as demonstrations against racism and police brutality continue," was a typical offering. "Children join parents to participate in #BlackLivesMatter march in New York," was another.

But when Cubans took to the streets of Havana to protest the communist government's failed economic policies, Reuters sang a different tune: "Cuban protests risk exacerbating COVID-19 spike."

10

"Antifa Is a Myth"

WHEN President Trump confronted Joe Biden at their first debate about Biden's refusal to forcefully condemn rioting, Biden artfully dodged the issue. He refused to denounce Antifa because, he said, he agreed with FBI Director Christopher Wray's assessment of the loose coalition of "anti-fascists" in the United States: "It's not an organization, it's an idea."

What I will say from personal observation is that Antifa may not be an official national organization, but it is something very much more than an "idea." Antifa is a real entity, even if it doesn't have the structure and bylaws of your local Rotary or Elks club.

And I can tell you that to the countless Americans who have had their businesses or vehicles destroyed, or were sent to the hospital bloody and broken after vicious attacks by its agitators, Antifa is more than an idea. It's a nightmare lived out in real life.

The Pacific Northwest offers the best example of the coalition of progressive protesters, pro-anarcho-communists, and "direct action" agitators who actively seek out and attack what they deem to be "fascist." They openly used Twitter to help coordinate gatherings that often turned violent. Of course, it's not just confined to Seattle or Portland. Antifa groups exist around the country, using social media to let people know where and when to gather in order to menace and intimidate.

Sure, they go by different names, but their goals and actions, down to what they wear, are all in line with the same movement. There is literally a group called Rose City Antifa in Portland, in addition to the

Pacific Northwest Youth Liberation Front. Washington, D.C. has the DC Youth Liberation Front. These groups have their slight differences and distinctions, largely geographical. But they are essentially all the same.

Antifa groups were not to blame for every single riot that occurred throughout 2020, but those involved with the movement often took advantage of any outrage if a city experienced multiple days of protest. If there was civil unrest they did not happen to start, they jumped in to amplify it.

Of course, not everyone appreciated that Antifa is effectively a domestic terrorist movement. MSNBC host Joy Reid tweeted, "If you're constantly yelling 'Antifa!'—which literally is short for 'anti-fascists,' ding-ding-ding!...you might be the fascist they're focused on. Just a thought..."[102]

The View cohost Joy Behar expressed a common stance held by conventional liberals, saying a particular Republican senator she wished to criticize is "scared of this fictitious idea of Antifa, a thing that doesn't even exist."[103]

Antifa does enjoy the support of some within the mainstream media, either because those journalists really are ignorant about the group's actions and motives, or they just don't care. For instance, Mara Liasson, a national political correspondent for NPR, tweeted that the D-Day landings were the "biggest antifa rally in history."[104] It got over 32,200 retweets and 133,800 likes. Whether Liasson was merely ignorant or was willfully being disingenuous about Antifa doesn't really matter.

We should dispel this notion of today's Antifa as the heirs and descendants of World War II veterans. Those who fought against Germany and Japan fought against real fascists who posed an actual threat to the world. They fought *for* freedom. By and large, they genuinely loved their country. They did not hate the United States nor wish for its downfall, which appears to be a central organizing principle for today's Antifa groups.

Hardcore Antifa activists babble endlessly about abolishing the US and installing some variation of anarcho-communism (whatever that is) in its place. The distinctions among various Antifa entities are usually so small—Marxist or Maoist? Anarchist or Nihilist?—as to be meaningless. These groups truly are all part of the same larger movement, which rejects everything the United States represents.

On social media and at gatherings, Antifa activists talk a big game about being "ungovernable" and how the "revolution" is close at hand.

As soon as they are met with force by police (usually well-deserved), they cry about violations of their rights—rights that are generally recognized by the very government they are trying to take violent action against!

Not having any central organization or leadership is one of Antifa's strengths. But it's also a major weakness. Time and time again, I saw whenever they were not busy attacking something or someone, Antifa members were arguing about what to do next or where to go.

The laziest misconception about the Antifa movement—the one put forth by Joy Reid—holds that if you're against them and their actions, well then, *you* are a fascist. After all, what they are about is clearly in the name, right?

It takes a lot of willful ignorance to make such a claim. It means ignoring the fact Antifa employs fascist tactics, like threats, intimidation, and actual violence, in a bid to achieve their goals. It means ignoring the fact that those goals—for the most part, the creation of a communist society—are themselves fascistic. There has never been a communist society that hasn't been totalitarian and fascistic. The very name "Antifa" is an Owellian smokescreen designed to obscure—not illuminate—the true ambitions of its adherents.

When I spoke with former Acting DHS Secretary Chad Wolf in February of 2021, I asked him what he thought about Christopher Wray's assessment of Antifa cited by Joe Biden. Wolf said those downplaying Antifa by calling it "an idea" or a "myth"—as Rep. Jerry Nadler (D-NY) did—are veering into "dangerous" territory.

Antifa "got very violent in Portland and other places," Wolf said. "Downplaying them and not calling them out, not holding them accountable, not prosecuting them only emboldens them."

Wolf added he believes the violence perpetrated by Antifa and similarly aligned groups that went on for months with little accountability helped spur others to violence. "You watch that and say, 'Okay well, if this group can do it, well then I can emulate that elsewhere.' And so, it sends a very bad signal that you need to address this. It doesn't matter if it's Antifa or if it's more right-wing folks that we saw on January 6th, you just got to call it out for what it is....There's no place in our society for that."

Antifa "was much more than an idea for our law enforcement officers there in Portland," Wolf said. "It was real, the violence was real. The organization, the finances that they had, all of that was real. It wasn't just a notion, it wasn't an idea, it wasn't made up, it wasn't spur of the moment....It was very, very coordinated."

Ken Cuccinelli, who served in a top position at DHS with Wolf, echoed that assessment.

"'[Antifa] have intentionally made themselves difficult to get your arms around, as a tactic, and it's proven effective," Cuccinelli told me. "They act as groups in Portland, they act as groups in Seattle and Chicago and so forth. Is it less formal than perhaps other things we've seen in the past? Sure, but that's a tactic. It's a tactic to avoid the kind of law enforcement attention that we're talking about here."

Like Wolf, Cuccinelli said the way to hold people involved in the Antifa movement and who commit criminal acts accountable is simple: Follow through on prosecuting them instead of playing catch-and-release.

If you do that, said Cuccinelli, you can use the conventional methods of combatting organized criminal outfits to put a dent in Antifa's ability to do harm. If you investigate and prosecute, then you can "determine through typical investigatory techniques where now you have probable cause, you have reasonable suspicion, you have all the elements to go up the chain of an investigation, what groups they were working with, what other people. If they are working with 10 or 20 people that don't have club meetings, they're still a group."

Prosecuting every individual involved in a riot that organized on social media and in private chats is easier said than done. That was certainly the case in Portland. Many serious cases, particularly those involving assaults on or around the federal courthouse, were prosecuted by the U.S. government. But those were at the federal level. In many other instances, Antifa groups would target local law enforcement and their facilities, since local officials in Portland and elsewhere have proven reluctant to fully prosecute offenders in such cases.

Even still, the U.S. Attorney's Office in Oregon dismissed many cases that were far more serious than simple trespassing or resisting arrest. A few examples:

- Thomas Johnson–Assault on a federal officer
- Jennifer Lynn Kristiansen–Assault on a federal officer
- Taylor Lemons–Assault on a federal officer
- Gabriel Huston–Assault on a federal officer

- Theodore O'Brien–Assault on a federal officer
- Benjamin Wood-Pavicich–Assault on a federal officer
- Pablo Avvacato–Assault on a federal officer
- Douglas Dean–Assault on a federal officer

The alleged assaults ranged from actions like using heavy objects, such as shields and helmets, to attack the officers, or using high-powered lasers to try to blind them, which can result in permanent blindness. By April of 2021, U.S. prosecutors had dismissed more than half of the 90 cases stemming from the month-long siege at the courthouse.[105]

Now compare those dismissals by federal prosecutors to the criminal cases against some of the January 6th rioters.

Take Paul Hodgkins, the first man convicted from the Capitol riot. He pleaded guilty to one count of obstructing an official proceeding after he walked onto the Senate floor carrying a "Trump 2020" flag. He was not accused or charged with assaulting police. He was not accused of causing any destruction of property. He had no prior criminal record.

The Justice Department argued Hodgkins should receive 18 months of prison time for breaching the Senate chamber. Federal prosecutors also said walking into the Senate chamber "was an act of domestic terrorism," even though, curiously, they did not charge him under any terrorism statutes.

The judge instead sentenced Hodgkins to eight months of jail time.[106]

I won't argue that any Capitol rioter—not even one as harmless as Paul Hodgkins—should be let off scot-free. Those who break the law should face the consequences. But it is hard to take the Justice Department seriously when it takes a tough stance against nonviolent offenders at the US Capitol while letting violent offenders from the federal courthouse in Portland slide.

It is not surprising the federal government cracked down harder on the Capitol rioters. The Capitol is a more significant location than a federal courthouse, and disrupting the proceedings of Congress in so consequential a matter as the certification of a presidential election cannot casually be tolerated.

But that logic doesn't mean that rioters at the federal courthouse in Portland—many of whom acted violently, in contrast to a lot of those prosecuted for their roles on January 6th—should be let off the hook either. The double standard only serves to widen the country's divisions.

Rioters should be held accountable in all instances, especially when their actions are violent and destructive. Failure to do so will only invite repeat offenses.

Federal prosecutors argued for throwing the book at Paul Hodgkins as a deterrent to future offenders. They're not wrong.

But the Department of Justice failed to apply the same logic in Portland. That *was* wrong.

ANTIFA AFTERMATH

The Justice Department's dismissal of federal charges against so many rioters at the federal courthouse in Portland was imprudent.

But the wholesale dismissal of charges against rioters by local prosecutors was, arguably, immoral.

Portland Police referred 1,108 criminal cases to the Multnomah District Attorney's Office between the start of the near constant rioting and protests in May and June of 2021. Prosecutors declined to file charges in 891 of those cases—more than 80 percent. Insufficient evidence was cited for just 108 dismissals. More than 700 were dismissed for reasons prosecutors said were "in the interest of justice."

"We look at every case individually and based on the merits," according to Multnomah County District Attorney Mike Schmidt. "We take into account who the individual is. We take into account what the severity of the harm is, if there's a victim in the case. We take into account the victim's input, so there really is not a one-size-fits-all system. We go to great lengths and great pain to tailor our resolutions to the specific of each individual and the facts of each case."

Of the 194 cases the DA's office decided to bring forward, only nine had been resolved one full year after the riots.[107] Most of those resulted in probation, not jail time.

It remains to be seen whether this approach will be sufficient to deter future Antifa violence in Portland. I sincerely doubt it.

11

After Action

NOTHING prepared me to report on the unrest our country experienced. It was all learning on the fly in the most intense situations I have ever been in. Sure, there were some fundamentals from the Marine Corps I could apply in a small number of situations, but riot coverage is a whole different ball game.

This is where I have to admit the constant internal battle I have with myself. Covering the riots across the country has been great for me. It's raised my profile and put money in my bank account. Heck, it's the reason I've been able to write a book.

What is hard about coming to terms with this success is that all of it is built off the backs of documenting people suffering what are often the worst days of their lives. Human suffering is something you never want to see happening anywhere, but it hurts even more to see when it's happening to your fellow countrymen, especially when they had nothing to do with what caused the outrage in the first place.

The way I view it, there are few who are willing to go into dangerous situations to accurately document what is really happening, keyword being accurately. If riots are going to happen, I might as well dive headfirst into the madness so the country can understand what is going on as it's happening in real-time. To observe, and to report, is to help understand. The suffering of so many innocent people as a result of rioters' actions would surely be compounded if no one ever learned the personal costs that riots have on a community.

Their stories deserve to be told because *all riots matter.*

Riot coverage gave me a sense of purpose. Anyone can "report" on just about any topic while sitting at home or in an office with a phone and an internet connection. But to go out and chew the dirt is much more fulfilling. This is a common feeling among my friends who cover riots as well. I wanted to transfer to Combat Camera while I was still in the reserves, but it never worked out so what was happening in the U.S. was the next best thing to fulfill my desire to document history.

That said, covering the chaos has come at a personal cost—a mental and physical toll that became pronounced by about August. My right knee started to feel pain from running around with so much gear on, sometimes for 12 hours a day or longer. A perfectly timed vacation after Kenosha helped, but I knew there were more riots waiting for me after I got back. In October, when things slowed down, I really started to feel the effects of post-traumatic stress.

After months of nonstop riot coverage, I started to have nightmares. The dreams and nightmares were so consistent it got to the point where I had one the very night after I was done covering a riot. Sometimes my dreams had me covering a riot in some vague city. Other times I'd wake up sweating with my heart racing. I began to dread going to sleep.

It is something I am somewhat ashamed to admit experiencing, considering I was not in any real warzone during my tour of America's 2020 battlegrounds. Add to this the fact I never deployed during my time in the reserves.

I know one is not supposed to compare traumatic events because trauma is trauma, but I was never starved, I was always in constant communication with people I cared about, I was always able to sleep in a bed after I was done being out in the field, and I was not out in the field for more than a week. Who was I to complain about "muh feelings" when I largely escaped serious injury, didn't have my business destroyed, and didn't have to clean up the mess the rioters left behind? Instead, I got to go on primetime national TV and had tweets that went viral.

It's why I made it a point to never compare wherever I was to an actual warzone. I knew no matter how difficult or dangerous my assignments were, it could have always been much worse.

"Why is this affecting me so much?"

I did not believe I "rated" to be experiencing the post-traumatic stress that close friends of mine who had deployed to Iraq and Afghanistan experienced. My situation was not comparable.

I was also aware that too many in my generation use claims of mental struggle as a crutch or a way to chase social media clout. I had to accept—and am still in the process of accepting, to be completely honest—the consequences from the stress of constantly traveling to places that were dangerous and threatening, even if they weren't Baghdad or Kabul.

More than that, I wanted to avoid making myself the story. I never wanted a "look how this is affecting me" moment, which certain narcissistic journalists love. I had enough sense to know that no one was tuning into my work because they wanted to know how I felt; they wanted to know what was happening.

I'm a reporter. I am not a hero, nor do I consider myself brave—stupid, perhaps, considering my willingness to consistently go back out into the field when I know the consequences of doing such work. After all, at the end of the day, I'm just a guy with a tape recorder and a camera.

My behavior changed as time went on. "I'd rather be at a riot" became an inside joke among my friends whenever I looked uninterested or disengaged at a gathering. As much as I dreaded covering episodes of urban unrest, I was always waiting for an opportunity to head back out into the fray.

I noticed I was less likely to post on Twitter other than to tweet an event I was covering. I had long thought that half the fun of being on Twitter was to put your political rivals on blast when they tweet a bad take. Before the riots, I would be more than happy to publicly dunk on someone who tweeted something I thought was stupid. After a while, that changed. Call it nihilism, apathy, or realizing Twitter arguments are largely a waste of time in the grand scheme of things, but after months of grueling work I would consider tweeting something in general and think, "What's the point?"

In the fall, I noticed I increasingly was using alcohol to take my mind off of what I had been through. While I never would drink to the point of blacking out (I hate puking and loathe waking up with a hangover) or drink alone, I would drink to mentally "cruise" when I was out with my friends so I'd go to bed still "cruising" in the hopes of not having a nightmare. It rarely worked.

The negative side effects of the work are hard to accept—not just the physical aches and pains, or the after-the-fact trauma, but the actual in-the-moment fear. On too many occasions I was very scared, terrified even, particularly when there was gunfire. (Perhaps unwisely, I never brought a firearm of my own to use in self-defense if the situation required it.)

Yet I very much enjoyed being in those chaotic situations. Riots are a free for all. You never know what may happen or what madness you'll run into. They gave me an adrenaline high. I imagine it was much the same for those hell-bent on destruction and mayhem. It's quite a rush.

It's a cliché to say I never felt more alive than when I was in the middle of some chaos in Portland or Kenosha or wherever. But it's true. And I would quickly grow bored when I got back home.

Covering the southern border crisis—my latest assignment since, fortunately, the unrest in America's cities has largely subsided—has given me a sense of purpose again in my reporting. But I'd be lying if I said it offered the same level of excitement. I guess I wanted to occupy my time in a major way to avoid having to think about the previous high-stress situations I had been in.

In the middle of working on this book, I was visiting Jared, a friend from Indiana Wesleyan University. His mother asked if writing down everything I had experienced was therapeutic. Not really, I told her. Having to really dig down to remember everything I'd witnessed just resulted in having the emotions attached to those often-bad memories come rushing to the surface. It's been more cathartic than therapeutic, a small but significant difference and even then, I'm not sure that would be the right word.

My conflicted feelings are best summed up in a conversation between Lt. Col. Stephen "Godfather" Ferrando and the Reporter in the last episode of the HBO miniseries *Generation Kill*. The show is based off the book of the same name by journalist Evan Wright, who was embedded with the Marine Corps' 1st Reconnaissance Battalion during the 2003 invasion of Iraq.

"But something else I'm struggling with…is the excitement I felt, getting shot at. It's something I had not anticipated about war. Did you?" Godfather asks the Reporter, who walks away without answering because, I assume, they both knew what he would say.

Again, I'm not trying to say I went to war, but when the shooting started in a riot, I felt an excitement and a fear that's hard to describe, replicate, and accept. It's a roller coaster of emotions that becomes addicting.

Not all of my behavior changes were negative. I have always prayed to God, whether in times of need or simply to maintain my connection to Him. Throughout 2020, I made it a priority to pray before heading out into a riot. While it was a standard "keep me safe from injury or death" prayer, I acknowledged whatever was going to happen was up to His will, active or passive, which was going to determine whether I was able to go home safely.

I'm also hesitant to talk about the mental toll from riot coverage, in part because of the online reaction to a *VICE* article about Capitol Hill reporters' experiences during the January 6th riot. Many Twitter users mocked the story. I had some people send me the article so I could dunk on *VICE*. Some of those quoted in the piece did seem a tad overdramatic or downright weird. Still, I couldn't bring myself to take a shot at them.[108]

I do understand these are Capitol Hill reporters, not street guys like myself or my fellow Riot Squad journalists at the *Daily Caller* and other publications. What is notable, however, is no one from a mainstream news outlet ever reached out to me to ask what I was going through mentally during the BLM riots. After all, how could I get post-traumatic stress from a riot that didn't really happen?

During the Capitol riot, I did have what felt like a panic attack after I escaped the suffocating sardine can in which I was nearly crushed to death. When I got outside, I found a small grassy lawn on which to catch my breath. I'm not a claustrophobic person, but what I had just gone through rattled me. The few other instances where I thought I might die in a riot lasted less than a minute. This incident lasted for almost 10 minutes.

It's hard to describe how distressing it was to feel trapped. In other circumstances, I had easy avenues of escape, but in the Capitol, there was nowhere to go as the panicked grew more packed. I wanted to quit covering riots entirely right then and there. In that moment, it felt as if all the stress and fear that had been building up for almost a full year, which I never fully processed, was going to mentally crush me.

"This is not worth it."

"That was stupid going in there."

"Why am I doing this?"

After getting control of my breathing and drinking some water, I was able to shake it off and get back to work. I don't include this for any sympathy points, but to show there is a cost to this work. At the same time, it is work I'm more than happy to do. It's an odd dynamic, I know.

As you can imagine, voluntarily putting myself in dangerous situations over and over again worried the people close to me. My mom told me that while she would be upset beyond belief, she would not be surprised in the slightest if I were killed covering a riot. She wanted me to understand that she had to brace herself for the worst since she understood the dangers of my chosen passion.

In September of 2020, I put in a request for Townhall to purchase level IV ceramic plates, which are rated to resist rifle rounds. I originally went with handgun plating because I was mostly concerned about getting shot again with a rubber bullet or some other crowd control round. If there were gunfire in the city, it would have most likely been handgun rounds anyway. The plating is also much lighter compared to level IV. I changed my mind after the Kenosha riots. After sending the email, it prompted a call from Jonathan Garthwaite, the head boss at Townhall Media.

"I just want you to know that you don't need to go to every one of these things," he told me. I appreciated the lack of pressure, I replied, but there's no other place I'd rather be.

"This is what I'm good at," I told him.

Over the course of the year, I got my fair share of messages from people I hadn't spoken to in years, asking if I was okay at whatever location I was in or telling me they saw one of my appearances on FOX News. The Capitol riot was the one where I got the most "Are you ok?" messages.

Another friend, an Army veteran, told me to stay away from fires after a pile of burning tires nearly toppled onto me in Kenosha. Fast forward to the Louisville riot. The same friend asked why I got near a trash fire only for an aerosol to explode right in front of me. I was lucky to avoid serious injury.

"It wasn't a tire fire," I said.

He laughed. "Marines, man, you have to tell them to stay away from black bears, brown bears, and grizzly bears. You can't just say stay away from bears!" Admittedly, he had a point.

I'm often asked how I would rank the riots I covered. It's an odd question. In some ways, the riots were all the same. In other ways, each was completely unique. And how would you rank them anyway? Best? Worst? Most fun? Most harrowing?

Starting with the absolute worst or most chaotic is difficult, but I would rank them as the following, taking into consideration total damage done, number of dead/injured, personal injuries/danger, and the significance of location:

1. Minneapolis
2. Kenosha
3. Capitol building
4. Portland (Federal Courthouse)
5. Philadelphia (October riot)
6. Louisville (September)
7. Washington, D.C. (Mid-June riots)
8. Wauwatosa
9. Seattle/CHAZ

From late May 2020 to early January 2021, I took at least 20 flights, not counting layovers. I was away from home almost every other week at the height of the insanity. Even when I didn't travel for a riot, I always had all of my gear with me because I never knew if something would pop off wherever I was.

A question I'm often asked is what I carry with me in my bag. It varied by day or location, but this is what I typically pack:

- Two water sources
- Two portable chargers with cables
- Notebook
- KA-BAR knife
- Business cards
- A small American flag
- A Bible
- A Solatac first aid kit

There were a few times I was identified at the different protests and riots I was covering by people I definitely did not want to recognize me. On my last day at CHAZ/CHOP, a young man walked up to me and asked if I had been on FOX News earlier in the week. I said no and walked away, thinking I had lost him. A few minutes later he found me again and showed me a YouTube video FOX News had posted of one of my appearances.

"This is you! You're wearing the same shirt!" the guy said.

I did not pack enough shirts, or even a jacket, on that trip because I did not anticipate being in Seattle all that long. Fortunately, he didn't make a big deal about it and blow my cover.

Another time during the Kenosha riots, a young woman overheard me giving a phone interview with a BBC radio station.

"Are you a fascist?!" the woman screamed at me while I was still on the phone.

I told her no while trying to walk away from her. I then had to explain to the radio host what the interruption was.

"We got a fascist over here!" the woman started to yell at the crowd. Thankfully, they were too preoccupied with fighting against the armored police vehicles to turn their attention to me.

The radio host then asked if I'd be willing to put the clearly deranged woman on the phone so he could interview her. I told the host I didn't think that would happen, but I'd try. The woman was still encouraging the other rioters to surround me, so I asked her if she wanted to talk to the BBC. She looked confused before finally walking away.

Other times when I was live tweeting a riot, Antifa-affiliated Twitter accounts would announce to their followers that I was in the area. That could make a tense situation even more harrowing, since nobody wants a target on his back. When I was in Louisville, an account belonging to Chad Loder tweeted to his tens of thousands of followers, "Julio Rosas, the fascist propagandist who lionized the Kenosha murder is on the ground at the #LouisvilleKY protests. If you see him, call him out."

Loder blocked my account, so I was unaware of this tweet. (Frankly, I was unaware who Loder was.) I only found out about it when some of my colleagues at PJ Media asked if it would be okay to write up the Chad Loder tweet. "What Chad Loder tweet?" I asked.

A friend sent me a screenshot of the tweet, which had been up for over four hours. Seeing how someone had already shot two police officers that evening, and who knew what could happen next, I decided to call it a night soon after.

It should go without saying—but I'll say it anyway—Loder's tweet was completely false. I never "lionized" Kyle Rittenhouse. I only stated what I saw in interviews after the shootings. As for being a "fascist propagandist," anyone or anything Antifa opposes is tarred as "fascist." Unless you're Joy Reid, it's impossible to take the claim seriously.

A small bit of good came from Loder's tweet, actually. Since it convinced me to pack things in early and leave, I avoided being arrested along with Shelby and Jorge. Had I stayed, I certainly would have gone with them to Louisville's Hall of Justice, where they were indiscriminately rounded up and arrested as part of a large crowd of protesters and rioters. So instead of spending a night in jail, I ate some Taco Bell and got some sleep in a real bed. Thanks Chad!

It would not be the last time Antifa or BLM sympathizers would tweet out my location to their followers. While they never explicitly stated I should be beaten up if I was found, that was definitely the goal.

Not every time I was recognized on the street was by agitators. The morning after the Wauwatosa riot, I visited a local coffee shop that had suffered damage. I hoped to get some breakfast along with an interview with the owners. While I was waiting for my order, a man came up to me and asked if I was the Julio Rosas who had been covering the night's craziness, unaware that he had noticed the Townhall Media logo on my quarter-zip that was same logo watermarked onto my videos.

"Depends," I replied. "Who's asking?" The man assured me he was not looking for trouble. He and his wife just wanted to thank me for covering the riot. The people at the outdoor table next to us overheard the conversation, and they said they had also seen my videos. They peppered me with questions about what I had seen and were even more intrigued when they realized I was the same Julio Rosas who had covered the riots in nearby Kenosha. What a pleasant change to meet people who were not looking to get in my face and yell at me!

AFTERMATH

If this is where you expect me to tell you what I think the solution is to solve our country's long-standing problems and prevent a repeat of the rampages and destruction we saw in 2020, well, I'm sorry. I'm not sure I have that answer.

There was a brief moment after Floyd's murder when nearly the entire country was unified in saying Derek Chauvin went too far and that a man died unnecessarily.

That unity began to fall apart after radical political activists decided the way to prevent another George Floyd incident was to defund the police.

In the wake of Chauvin's actions, there was a legitimate need for a national discussion on proper policing. But demonizing all police officers and calling on police departments to be defunded and/or abolished served only to poison that discussion before it could even take place. And pushing such a foolish idea, ironically, has only served to make things worse for communities of color around the country.

What is particularly disturbing and even telling about the state of trust in the justice system is *when* the riots in 2020 broke out. The 1992 Los Angeles riots commenced only after police officers involved in the Rodney King case were largely let off the hook for the beating they gave him, not in the immediate aftermath of that beating.

Fast forward nearly 30 years, with more controversial police actions and misconduct added to the mix, the breakdown in society was immediate, widespread, and constant. Rioting began very shortly after Floyd's death. This was accelerated in part by the ability of news and videos to fly on social media. But it also represents an unwillingness by people to let the justice system take its course. Often forgotten is that Chauvin and his fellow officers were immediately fired after the incident, after all, and Chauvin ultimately was convicted. (The other officers' trials have not taken place as of publication.)

It was also disturbing to see how just the threat of riots could turn a town of any size on its head.

Take the small hamlet of Elizabeth City, North Carolina, which I visited in April 2021. The Pasquotank County Sheriff's Department was under intense scrutiny following the shooting death of Andrew Brown Jr., a black man, by sheriff deputies serving a drug search warrant.

With a population of just under 20,000 people, the small town had been thrust into the national spotlight in a way that had become all too familiar over the previous 11 months. One reason Elizabeth City was on edge was because the body camera footage of the incident had been withheld from the public.

I arrived in the city during the evening to find loud but peaceful protests. The entire city was preparing for the worst, expecting the night to turn violent like in so many other locales. Business owners had boarded up storefront windows. Roads were blocked off. Most importantly, police were stationed *everywhere.*

No major rioting occurred in Elizabeth City while I was there. One could almost hear the city's collective sigh of relief. It was clear residents felt they had gotten lucky—and maybe they had. Perhaps the city's small population helped limit troubles, not to mention that the nearest metro-politan area, Norfolk/Virginia Beach, was an hour away.

But it was also clear to me that having a significant police presence—and showing a willingness to act to protect civil order—would go a long way toward keeping the entire community safe.

The next morning I went for breakfast at a local diner located near the sheriff's department. The place was empty save for one customer taking an order to go. Employees said business had been so slow all morning they were going to close early. The lack of customers, they said, was due to a combination of roads being blocked off and people worried about heading downtown.

That was unfortunate, I thought, but far preferable to the scenes I had seen play out in so many other cities and towns.

I do not know what the future holds, only that I will continue to go wherever the next major riot occurs—assuming one occurs—for as long as I'm able to.

But I sincerely hope I never have to drop everything, strap on my gear, and hop on the next plane to chronicle scenes of urban warfare.

I hope we've learned some lessons about how to protect our citizens and their homes and businesses from the senseless destruction visited on our cities by a lunatic fringe.

It seems like Elizabeth City, North Carolina, was able to figure it out. With luck, officials in other towns and cities—mayors, city council members, police chiefs, prosecutors, and others—have learned something from America's 2020 crackup as well.

After all, as the saying goes, there are no winners in riots, only survivors.

ACKNOWLEDGEMENTS

THIS is where I want to thank everyone who helped produced this book and for providing support during my travels. Without them and many more, this book would not have happened:

My Mom and Dad; my bosses and coworkers at Townhall.com, past and present: Katie Pavlich, Jonathan Garthwrite, Guy Benson, Storm Paglia, Matt Vespa, Spencer Brown, Reagan McCarthy, Cortney O'Brien, Micah Rate, Bronson Stocking, Leah Barkoukis, and Beth Baumann; the rest of the Townhall Media family; Daily Caller friends: Logan Hall, Greg Price, Richie McGinniss, Shelby Talcott, Jorge Ventura, and Phillip Nieto; The Blaze friends: Elijah Schaffer and Savanah Hernandez; fellow riot/protest reporters: Mike Tobin, Geoff Nelson, Brendan Gutenschwager, Kalen, James Klüg, and Jason Rantz; my riot gear providers: Grunt Style (shirts and outerwear), Sakar Tactical (handgun/rifle plates and ballistic helmet), and Solatac (first aid kit); the media giants who helped elevate my reporting when I was lesser-known: Tucker Carlson, Laura Ingraham, Shannon Bream, their production staff, Brian Flood, Dana Loesch, Cam Edwards, and Ben Shapiro; friends: Chase Woodall, Kyle Hooten, Kevin McMahon, Caleb Joy, Curtis Houck, Nick Solheim, Sam Rodgers, and the Goons. Last but certainly not least: God, for keeping me "mostly" safe (the rubber bullet hit could have been much worse).

NOTES

CHAPTER 1

1. Tracker, U. P. (2020, May 30). *Dozens of journalists say they were targeted with tear gas, projectiles during Minneapolis protests*. Retrieved from https://pressfreedomtracker.us/all-incidents/police-target-dozens-journalists-covering-protests-minneapolis-tear-gas-pepper-spray-rubber-bullets/

2. Chuculate, E. (2020, May 29). *Fire during Minneapolis riots guts Native youth nonprofit*. Retrieved from indiancountrytoday.com: https://indiancountrytoday.com/news/fire-during-minneapolis-riots-guts-native-youth-nonprofit?redir=1

3. Meitrodt, J. (2020, June 6). Retrieved from Star Tribune: https://www.startribune.com/twin-cities-rebuilding-begins-with-donations-pressure-on-government/571075592/?refresh=true

4. Melvin, C. (2020, May 28). Retrieved from Twitter: https://twitter.com/craigmelvin/status/1266030830473940993

5. Alcindor, Y. (2020, May 31). Retrieved from Twitter: https://twitter.com/Yamiche/status/1267192733535555585

CHAPTER 2

6. lizpleasant. (2020, June). Retrieved from https://twitter.com/lizpleasant/status/1271223532953862144

7. Breezy_takeitEZ. (2020, May). Retrieved from Twitter: https://twitter.com/Breezy_takeitEZ/status/1271973878441472000

8. Julio_Rosas11. (2020, June 13). Retrieved from Twitter: https://twitter.com/Julio_Rosas11/status/1271986603620098048

9. Furfaro, H. (2020, June 22). Retrieved from Seattle Times: https://www.seattletimes.com/seattle-news/teen-who-died-in-chop-shooting-wanted-to-be-loved-those-who-knew-him-recall/

10. Rantz, J. (2020, December 11). Retrieved from MyNorthWest: https://mynorthwest.com/2358938/rantz-33-officers-leave-seattle-police-mass-exodus/

11. Hughes, T. (2020, June 14). *In Seattle's Capitol Hill autonomous protest zone, some Black leaders express doubt about white allies*. Retrieved from usatoday.com: https://www.usatoday.com/story/news/nation/2020/06/14/inside-seattle-autonomous-zone-black-protesters-seek-lasting-change/3179232001/

12. Scigliano, E. (2020, June 15). *Don't Listen to Fox. Here's What's Really Going On in Seattle's Protest Zone*. Retrieved from politico.com: https://www.politico.com/news/magazine/2020/06/15/dont-listen-to-fox-heres-whats-really-going-on-in-seattles-protest-zone-321507

13. Royale, R. (2020, June 19). *Seattle's Autonomous Zone Is Not What You've Been Told*. Retrieved from rollingstone.com: https://www.rollingstone.com/culture/culture-features/chop-chaz-seattle-autonomous-zone-inside-protests-1017637/

14. KING5. (2020, June 23). *Man injured in third Capitol Hill shooting since Saturday.* Retrieved from www.king5.com: https://www.king5.com/article/news/local/seattle/seattle-police-investigate-capitol-hill-shooting/281-04c066b5-e492-4441-a5a5-cd5805144238

CHAPTER 3

15. Department of Justice, U. A. (2020, July 31). *Portland Man Charged in July 28, 2020 Arson at Mark O. Hatfield U.S. Courthouse.* Retrieved from Department of Justice: https://www.justice.gov/usao-or/pr/portland-man-charged-july-28-2020-arson-mark-o-hatfield-us-courthouse

16. N'dea Yancey-Bragg, K. P. (2020, July 17). *'Secret police force': Feds reportedly pull Portland protesters into unmarked vehicles, stirring outrage.* Retrieved from USA Today: https://www.usatoday.com/story/news/nation/2020/07/17/reports-federal-officers-detain-portland-protesters-unmarked-vans/5457471002/

17. Lead, T. (2020, July 17). *Mysterious arrest video with unidentified police raises questions.* Retrieved from CNN: https://www.cnn.com/videos/politics/2020/07/17/unidentified-police-arrests-oregon-lead-vpx.cnn

18. Ward, A. (2020, July 20). *The unmarked federal agents arresting people in Portland, explained.* Retrieved from Vox: https://www.vox.com/2020/7/20/21328387/portland-protests-unmarked-arrest-trump-wold

19. Danner, A. K. (2020, July 17). *Unidentified Federal Agents Are Detaining Protesters in Portland.* Retrieved from New York Magazine: https://nymag.com/intelligencer/2020/07/unidentified-federal-agents-detaining-protesters-in-portland.html

20. Pelosi, N. (2020, July 17). Retrieved from Twitter: https://twitter.com/speakerpelosi/status/1284294427654197248?lang=en

21. Wyden, R. (2020, July 16). Retrieved from Twitter: https://twitter.com/RonWyden/status/1283868641549848584

22. Wheeler, T. (2020, July 21). Retrieved from Twitter: https://twitter.com/tedwheeler/status/1285717823248044032

23. Rosas, J. (2002, August 4). *Ted Cruz Corrects Mazie Hirono On the Spot After Falsely Claiming Federal Agents Were 'Unidentifiable'.* Retrieved from Townhall: https://townhall.com/tipsheet/juliorosas/2020/08/04/ted-cruz-corrects-mazie-hirono-on-the-spot-after-falsely-claiming-federal-agents-were-unidentifiable-n2573716

24. Kristof, N. (2020, July 23). Retrieved from Twitter: https://twitter.com/NickKristof/status/1286166223357714434

25. Rosas, J. (2020, August 6). *'It's Outrageous': CBP Commissioner Shreds 'Lying' Dems Still Claiming DHS Agents Were 'Unidentifiable'.* Retrieved from Townhall: https://townhall.com/tipsheet/juliorosas/2020/08/06/it-outrageous-cbp-commissioner-shreds-lying-dems-still-claiming-dhs-agents-were-unidentifiable-n2573876

26. Police, P. (2020, August 7). Retrieved from Twitter: https://twitter.com/PortlandPolice/status/1291607391633473536

27. FromKalen. (2020, August 17). Retrieved from Twitter: https://twitter.com/FromKalen/status/1295245694177951748

28. Eustachewich, L. (2020, August 19). *Here's what we know about alleged attacker Marquise Love in Portland beatdown.* Retrieved from New York Post: https://

nypost.com/2020/08/19/heres-what-we-know-about-portland-attacker-marquise-love/

29. KOIN6. (2021, January 1). *Wheeler calls out 'antifa anarchists' following NYE riot.* Retrieved from KOIN.com: https://www.koin.com/local/multnomah-county/wheeler-ppb-chief-to-hold-virtual-press-conference/

CHAPTER 4

30. Rosas, J. (2020, August 25). *Kenosha Business Owners and Residents Speak Out After Rioters Destroy Buildings In Night of Chaos.* Retrieved from Townhall. com: https://townhall.com/tipsheet/juliorosas/2020/08/25/kenosha-business-owners-and-residents-speak-out-after-rioters-destroy-buildings-in-another-night-of-chaos-n2575006

31. Richman, J. (2020, August 27). *https://www.jns.org/amid-riots-synagogue-in-kenosha-wis-vandalized-with-free-palestine/.* Retrieved from jns.org: https://www.jns.org/amid-riots-synagogue-in-kenosha-wis-vandalized-with-free-palestine/

32. Jaffe, R. K. (2020, October 3). *A mentally ill man, a heavily armed teenager and the night Kenosha burned.* Retrieved from washingtonpost.com: https://www.washingtonpost.com/nation/2020/10/03/kenosha-shooting-victims/?arc404=true

33. Vielmetti, B. (2020, October 15). *Kenosha protester charged with firing gun right before Kyle Rittenhouse began shooting.* Retrieved from jsonline.com: https://www.jsonline.com/story/news/crime/2020/10/15/kenosha-protester-charged-firing-gun-prior-rittenhouse-shots/3667399001/

34. AntifaWatch2. (2020, August 29). Retrieved from Twitter: https://twitter.com/AntifaWatch2/status/1299853616757583872

35. BGOnTheScene. (2020, August 26). Retrieved from Twitter: https://twitter.com/bgonthescene/status/1298502384654651392

36. Bauer, S. G. (2020, August 27). *17-year-old arrested after 2 killed during unrest in Kenosha.* Retrieved from ap.com: https://apnews.com/article/ap-top-news-racial-injustice-il-state-wire-shootings-wi-state-wire-97a0700564fb52d7f66 4d8de22066f88

37. Joyce Sohyun Lee, R. O. (2020, November 19). *Kenosha: How two men's paths crossed in an encounter that has divided the nation.* Retrieved from washingtonpost.com: https://www.washingtonpost.com/investigations/2020/11/19/kenosha-shooting-kyle-rittenhouse-interview/

38. Caller, D. (2020, August 26). *Alleged Kenosha Shooter Spoke With Daily Caller Before Fatal Incident.* Retrieved from YouTube.com: https://www.youtube.com/watch?v=kYb7loD7RGg

CHAPTER 5

39. Hickey, M. (2020, August 27). *Owner Of Burned Kenosha Mattress Store Reunites Man Who Risked His Life Tried To Save It.* Retrieved from chicago.cbslocal.com: https://chicago.cbslocal.com/2020/08/27/owner-of-burned-kenosha-mattress-store-reunites-man-who-risked-his-life-tried-to-save-it/

CHAPTER 6

40. Wisconsin, U. A. (2021, July 13). *Multiple Men Indicted for Arson and Other Offenses Committed During Unrest in Kenosha; Investigation Into Other Suspects*

Continues. Retrieved from justice.gov: https://www.justice.gov/usao-edwi/pr/
multiple-men-indicted-arson-and-other-offenses-committed-during-unrest-kenosha

41. Wamsley, L. (2021, January 15). *What We Know So Far: A Timeline Of Security
Response At The Capitol On Jan. 6*. Retrieved from npr.com: https://www.npr.
org/2021/01/15/956842958/what-we-know-so-far-a-timeline-of-security-at-the-
capitol-on-january-6

42. tomselliott. (2021, February 11). Retrieved from Twitter.com: https://twitter.com/
tomselliott/status/1359915611321757697

43. cspan. (2021, January 7). Retrieved from Twitter: https://twitter.com/cspan/
status/1347272949284425728

44. Tibbetts, M. (2020, June 1). *National World War II Memorial Vandalized*. Retrieved
from military.com: https://www.military.com/daily-news/2020/06/01/national-
world-war-ii-memorial-vandalized.html

45. Pelosi, N. (2020, June 4). *Pelosi Sends Letter to President Trump on Deployment of
Troops & Unidentified Law Enforcement Personnel in Nation's Capital*. Retrieved
from speaker.gov: https://www.speaker.gov/newsroom/6420-0

46. Johnson, A. (2021, January 11). *OLYMPIC GOLD MEDALIST KLETE KELLER
IN US CAPITOL DURING CLASHES, VIDEO SHOWS*. Retrieved from
swimswam.com: swimswam.com/olympic-gold-medalist-in-us-capitol-during-
clashes-video-appears-to-show/

CHAPTER 7

47. Re, G. (2020, January 19). *NBC News' Ben Collins slammed for warning of 'white
nationalist rally in Virginia'*. Retrieved from foxnews.com: https://www.foxnews.
com/media/nbc-ben-collins-virginia-white-nationalist-rally-guns

48. JerylBier. (2020, January 20). Retrieved from Twitter: https://twitter.com/JerylBier/
status/1219297330387701760

49. Eustachewich, L. (2018, June 26). *New Yorker staffer resigns after falsely accusing
ICE agent of having Nazi tattoo*. Retrieved from newyorker.com: https://nypost.
com/2018/06/26/new-yorker-staffer-resigns-after-falsely-accusing-ice-agent-of-
having-nazi-tattoo/

50. oliverdarcy. (2020, June 11). Retrieved from Twitter: https://twitter.com/oliverdarcy/
status/1271161342217650176

51. washingtonpost. (2020, August 25). Retrieved from Twitter: https://twitter.com/
washingtonpost/status/1298210231026098177

52. cnnbrk. (2020, August 24). Retrieved from Twitter: https://twitter.com/cnnbrk/
status/1297999965235617793

53. espn. (2020, August 24). Retrieved from Twitter: https://twitter.com/espn/
status/1297968681595613184

54. Reuters. (2020, August 25). Retrieved from Twitter: https://twitter.com/Reuters/
status/1298378367901659138

55. politico. (2020, August 26). Retrieved from Twitter: https://twitter.com/politico/
status/1298726917173129217

56. Wulfsohn, J. (2021, January 5). *Washington Post slammed for claiming Jacob Blake
was 'unarmed' during altercation with Kenosha police*. Retrieved from foxnews.
com: https://www.foxnews.com/media/washington-post-jacob-blake-unarmed-
kenosha

57. BGOnTheScene. (2020, September 23). Retrieved from Twitter: https://twitter.com/BGOnTheScene/status/1308856839287824384

58. Reuters. (2020, September 23). Retrieved from Twitter: https://twitter.com/Reuters/status/1308948243187937280

59. BrandyZadrozny. (2020, August 21). Retrieved from Twitter: https://twitter.com/BrandyZadrozny/status/1296885028182470657

60. Wulfsohn, J. (2020, September 1). CNN *reporter blasted for tweet downplaying Portland violence: 'The city is not under siege'*. Retrieved from foxnews.com: https://www.foxnews.com/media/cnn-josh-campbell-tweet-portland

61. Rosas, J. (2020, August 4). *Portland Rioters Set Their Sights on Another Target After Feds Begin Withdrawing from Courthouse*. Retrieved from Townhall: https://townhall.com/tipsheet/juliorosas/2020/08/04/portland-rioters-set-their-sights-on-another-target-after-feds-begin-withdrawing-from-courthouse-n2573669

62. Cilliza, C. (2020, August 31). *'Protests' or 'riots?' It makes a BIG difference*. Retrieved from cnn.com: https://www.cnn.com/2020/08/30/politics/us-election-2020-week-ahead/index.html

63. Bowles, N. (2020, September 21). *Some Protests Against Police Brutality Take a More Confrontational Approach*. Retrieved from nytimes.com: https://www.nytimes.com/2020/09/21/us/black-lives-matter-protests-tactics.html

64. ScooterCasterNY. (2020, September 4). Retrieved from Twitter: https://twitter.com/ScooterCasterNY/status/1302060108898357257

65. Morales, E. C. (2020, October 7). *Milwaukee County district attorney will not charge Police Officer Joseph Mensah in shooting death of Alvin Cole*. Retrieved from jsonline.com: https://www.jsonline.com/story/communities/west/news/wauwatosa/2020/10/07/wauwatosa-police-officer-joseph-mensah-da-decision-coming/3446512001/

66. Rosas, J. (2020, October 8). *Wisconsin Residents React to Damage Caused to Homes and Businesses During Chaotic Night In Wauwatosa*. Retrieved from Townhall.com: https://townhall.com/tipsheet/juliorosas/2020/10/08/wauwatosa-becomes-latest-american-town-where-mobs-cause-damage-n2577725

67. Hains, T. (2020, June 4). *CNN's Chris Cuomo: Who Says Protests Are Supposed To Be Polite And Peaceful?* Retrieved from realclearpolitics.com: https://www.realclearpolitics.com/video/2020/06/04/cnns_chris_cuomo_who_says_protests_are_supposed.html

68. paulkrugman. (2021, April 22). Retrieved from Twitter: https://twitter.com/paulkrugman/status/1385216421236510720

69. paulwaldman1. (2021, April 21). Retrieved from Twitter: https://twitter.com/paulwaldman1/status/1385025629444317185

70. Medina, J. (2021, March 5). *A Vexing Question for Democrats: What Drives Latino Men to Republicans?* Retrieved from nytimes.com: https://www.nytimes.com/2021/03/05/us/politics/latino-voters-democrats.html

71. Herndon, A. (2021, January 17). *How Republicans Are Warping Reality Around the Capitol Attack*. Retrieved from nytimes.com: https://www.nytimes.com/2021/01/17/us/politics/Capitol-conspiracy-theories-blm-antifa.html

72. Healy, P. (2021, May 21). *14 Trump Voters on the Legacy of George Floyd*. Retrieved from nytimes.com: https://www.nytimes.com/2021/05/21/opinion/conservatives-race-blm-floyd.html

73. Mackey, R. (2021, May 13). *MEET THE RIOT SQUAD: RIGHT-WING REPORTERS WHOSE VIRAL VIDEOS ARE USED TO SMEAR BLM.* Retrieved from theintercept.com: https://theintercept.com/2021/05/13/riot-squad-right-wing-video-journalists-black-lives-matter-antifa/

74. ryanjreilly. (2021, May 13). Retrieved from Twitter: https://twitter.com/ryanjreilly/status/1392996008544583686

CHAPTER 8

75. Overhultz, L. (2020, August 11). *Here Are The Celebrities Who Donated To Minnesota Freedom Fund, Which Bailed Out Several Allegedly Violent Criminals.* Retrieved from dailycaller.com: https://dailycaller.com/2020/08/11/seth-rogen-steve-carrell-celebrities-minnesota-freedom-fund-donations-george-floyd-protests/

76. KamalaHarris. (2020, June 1). Retrieved from Twitter: https://twitter.com/KamalaHarris/status/1267555018128965643

77. lululemon. (2020, May 29). Retrieved from instagram.com: https://www.instagram.com/p/CAy3PtKJOdN/?utm_source=ig_embed

78. Lyden, T. (2020, August 9). *Minnesota nonprofit with $35M bails out those accused of violent crimes.* Retrieved from fox9.com: https://www.fox9.com/news/minnesota-nonprofit-with-35m-bails-out-those-accused-of-violent-crimes

79. Lyman, B. (2021, February 2). *Harris-Backed Bail Fund Freed Rioter Twice. He's Now Charged With 3 New Felonies.* Retrieved from dailycaller.com: https://dailycaller.com/2021/02/02/minnesota-freedom-fund-bailed-thomas-moseley-three-felony-charges-gun-investigation/

80. Concha, J. (2020, August 20). *CNN's Lemon warns of Democratic 'blind spot' on 'riots': 'It shows up in the polling'.* Retrieved from thehill.com: https://thehill.com/homenews/media/513742-cnns-lemon-warns-of-democratic-blind-spot-on-riots-it-shows-up-in-the-polling

81. Biden, J. (2020, October 6). *Michelle Obama's Closing Argument | Joe Biden For President 2020.* Retrieved from Youtube.com: https://www.youtube.com/watch?v=5l_Xz2MIh4s&t=3s

82. IlhanMN. (2020, August 24). Retrieved from Twitter.com: https://twitter.com/IlhanMN/status/1297944866563985408

83. RepSwalwell. (2020, August 24). Retrieved from Twitter.com: https://twitter.com/RepSwalwell/status/1297923888744148995

84. chicagosmayor. (2020, August 24). Retrieved from Twitter.com: https://twitter.com/chicagosmayor/status/1297882815011459076

85. SenatorDurbin. (2020, August 25). Retrieved from Twitter.com: https://twitter.com/SenatorDurbin/status/1298319425230209025

86. NBCChicago. (2020, August 11). *Black Lives Matter on Chicago Looting: Black Lives 'More Important Than Downtown Corporations'.* Retrieved from nbcchicago.com: https://www.nbcchicago.com/news/local/black-lives-matter-on-chicago-looting-black-lives-more-important-than-downtown-corporations/2320685/

87. Stimson, B. (2020, August 13). *Ronald McDonald House in Chicago vandalized by looters.* Retrieved from https://www.foxnews.com/us/ronald-mcdonald-house-in-chicago-vadalized-by-looters

88. Bowles, N. (2020, November 9). *Businesses Trying to Rebound After Unrest Face a Challenge: Not Enough Insurance*. Retrieved from nytimes.com: https://www.nytimes.com/2020/11/09/business/small-business-insurance-unrest-kenosha.html

89. Jones, D. R. (2020). *Demonstrations & Political Violence in America*. Armed Conflict Location & Event Data Project.

90. Rosas, J. (2020, September 8). *Seattle Rioters Attacked Police Officers with Molotov Cocktails and Projectiles During Labor Day Unrest*. Retrieved from Townhall.com: https://townhall.com/tipsheet/juliorosas/2020/09/08/seattle-police-arrest-22-rioters-after-molotov-cocktails-and-projectiles-are-thrown-at-them-n2575793

91. Medvin, M. (2020, June 15). *The Atlanta Wendy's Officer Shooting: Justified Use of Force*. Retrieved from Townhall.com: https://townhall.com/columnists/marinamedvin/2020/06/15/the-atlanta-wendys-officer-shooting--justified-use-of-force-n2570674

92. Bureau, P. P. (2021). *Protests in Portland*. Retrieved from www.portlandoregon.gov: https://www.portlandoregon.gov/police/article/783250

93. Anderson, C. (2020, June 25). *House Dems Unanimously Block Resolution Condemning Violence and Rioting*. Retrieved from freebeacon.com: https://freebeacon.com/elections/house-dems-unanimously-block-resolution-condemning-violence-and-rioting/

94. Pavlich, K. (2021, April 19). *Documents show Maxine Waters requested police escort*. Retrieved from: https://townhall.com/tipsheet/katiepavlich/2021/04/19/documents-show-maxine-waters-requested-police-escort-before-screed-advocating-for-violence-n2588144

CHAPTER 9

95. Saad, L. (2020, August 5). *Black Americans Want Police to Retain Local Presence*. Retrieved from news.gallup.com: https://news.gallup.com/poll/316571/black-americans-police-retain-local-presence.aspx

96. Susan Page, D. A. (2021, July 25). *Exclusive poll finds Detroit residents far more worried about public safety than police reform*. Retrieved from usatoday.com: https://www.usatoday.com/story/news/politics/2021/07/25/detroit-police-reform-public-safety-defund-suffolk-poll/8001468002/

97. Minnesota, T. (2021, May 26). *The Truth Revealed about BLM*. Retrieved from Youtube.com: https://www.youtube.com/watch?v=wncYj2xfV6A

98. Police, U. P. (2020, June 24). *ATTEMPT TO IDENTIFY*. Retrieved from scribd.com: https://www.scribd.com/document/467238395/6-25-20-Jackson-BOLOs

99. Jones, C. (2020, June 22). *WATCH: Seattle's autonomous zone had a segregated black-only zone—and it was guarded by white people*. Retrieved from thepostmillennial.com: https://thepostmillennial.com/watch-seattles-autonomous-zone-has-a-segregated-black-only-zone-and-its-guarded-by-white-people

100. GovWhitmer. (2020, November 24). Retrieved from Twitter.com: https://twitter.com/GovWhitmer/status/1331366697224310786

101. Ducharme, J. (2020, June 10). *'Protest Is a Profound Public Health Intervention.' Why So Many Doctors Are Supporting Protests in the Middle of the COVID-19 Pandemic*. Retrieved from Time Magazine: https://time.com/5848212/doctors-supporting-protests/

CHAPTER 10

102. JoyAnnReid. (2021, July 18). Retrieved from Twitter.com: https://twitter.com/ JoyAnnReid/status/1416834404362686475

103. Justice, T. (2021, March 15). *'The View' Co-Host Joy Behar Claims Antifa 'Doesn't Even Exist'*. Retrieved from thefederalist.com: https://thefederalist. com/2021/03/15/the-view-co-host-joy-behar-claims-antifa-doesnt-even-exist/

104. MaraLiasson. (2020, June 6). Retrieved from Twitter.com: https://twitter.com/ MaraLiasson/status/1269390712291893248

105. AntifaWatch2. (2020, December 3). Retrieved from Twitter.com: https://twitter.com/ AntifaWatch2/status/1334666182205566976

106. Cohen, M. (2021, July 20). *First US Capitol rioter convicted of a felony gets 8 months in prison after DOJ says stiffer sentence could stop future attacks.* Retrieved from cnn.com: https://www.cnn.com/2021/07/19/politics/capitol-riot-felony-paul-hodgkins/index.html

107. Kavanaugh, S. D. (2020, October 7). *Multnomah County DA declines to prosecute 70% of Portland protest cases.* Retrieved from oregonlive.com: https://www. oregonlive.com/news/2020/10/multnomah-county-da-declines-to-prosecute-70-of-portland-protest-cases.html

CHAPTER 11

108. Joseph, C. (2021, July 6). *'So, So Angry': Reporters Who Survived the Capitol Riot Are Still Struggling.* Retrieved from vice.com: https://www.vice.com/en/ article/4avqqn/reporters-survived-capitol-riot-struggling